TRANSMUTATION

— AND THE —

HUMAN

CONSCIOUSNESS

TRANSMUTATION
─── AND THE ───
HUMAN
CONSCIOUSNESS

ANN EDGECLIFF

ARCHWAY PUBLISHING

Archway Publishing books may be ordered through booksellers or by contacting:

Archway Publishing
1663 Liberty Drive
Bloomington, IN 47403
www.archwaypublishing.com
844-669-3957

ISBN: 978-1-6657-5695-2 (sc)
ISBN: 978-1-6657-5697-6 (hc)
ISBN: 978-1-6657-5696-9 (e)

Library of Congress Control Number: 2024903686

Print information available on the last page.

Archway Publishing rev. date: 04/18/2024

DISCLAIMER

The content of this spiritual book is intended for informational purposes only. It does not constitute professional advice, and the author is not liable for any actions taken by readers based on the information provided within these pages.

The views, opinions, and beliefs expressed in this book are those of the author. Additionally, the author acknowledges that spirituality is a deeply personal and subjective journey, and readers are encouraged to explore various perspectives and interpretations.

Furthermore, this book may contain references to religious or cultural beliefs that some readers may find controversial or conflicting with their own beliefs. Readers are advised to approach such content with an open mind and respectful curiosity.

By reading this book, readers agree to take full responsibility for their actions and decisions, and they release the author from any liability arising from the use or misuse of the information presented herein.

Finally, the practices and teachings shared in this book are not intended to replace or substitute for any religious, medical, or psychological advice or treatment. Each individual is encouraged to discern what resonates with his or her own truth and to seek guidance accordingly.

Thank you for your understanding and may your spiritual journey be filled with light, love, and growth.

This book is dedicated to my parents and to my sister, Chrissy.

I would like to thank my mentor, Cindy Riggs. I could not have written this book without your input and suggestions. I would also like to thank some close friends who have supported and helped me in not only writing this book, but also in the journey of life. So, thank you to Kris H., Nic Lee, and TZ. You all mean the world to me.

INTRODUCTION

One of the most thought-about topics is death. What happens when you die? Where do you go? How does it feel? Would it surprise you to know that each of these questions has more than one answer? Preparing for the best possible transition (i.e., reuniting with your divine self peacefully and without what humans would call fear) involves preparation. And that is what this book is designed to do—to help you achieve transmutation by preparing your body and spirit while you are on this plane. You will do this by picking one or more of the eleven guides in this book. (These particular beings have agreed to assist and guide your human consciousness with transmutation and to participate in this book.) Before introducing you to the specific guides, though, there are a few topics to cover.

Most (if not all) religions come down to the underlying themes of comfort, guidance, and love. These underlying messages are universal. As humans, we seem to divide ourselves by seeking guidance from one particular religion. Some humans take the stance of having no religious beliefs at all. But there is guidance to be had from all of them (even not taking a stance). We are all energy. And in death, our energy does not just stop. Energy is not destroyed; it just takes another form. It converts (or transmutes) from one type of energy into another. That transition may be difficult for some. It may perhaps also be feared. This book is meant to ease the reader's fear by creating a relationship between the reader and one or more of the specific energies who have agreed to participate.

This book will be transcribed by a person who is channeling the energies that make up this book. In order to channel, the transcriptionist connects with the energies and allows them to speak through her. (The transcriptionist is female.) She has been a student for over fifteen years and has learned to channel through many years of practice. As the reader, you will not be channeling (unless you already know how to do so), but you will be opening yourself up to feeling these energies.

Anubis has requested to be the narrator. He is the Egyptian god of death, mummification, embalming, the afterlife, cemeteries, tombs, and the underworld. He is usually depicted as a canine or a man with a canine head. Anubis was a protector of graves and cemeteries. One of the roles of Anubis was the guardian of the scales. This is the critical scene depicting the weighing of the heart in the Book of the Dead. It shows Anubis performing a measurement that determined whether the person was worthy of entering the realm of the dead (the underworld, known as Duat). By weighing the heart of a deceased person against *ma'at* (or truth), which was often represented as an ostrich feather, Anubis dictated the fate of souls. Souls heavier than a feather would be devoured by Ammit, and souls lighter than a feather would ascend to a heavenly existence. He would like to say a few words to introduce himself and the purpose and power of this book.

ANUBIS

Greetings, humans. I thank you for giving me the floor and allowing me to narrate this journey. You see, while some of us have been around the block (as you would say), we have not had too many interactions with humans these days. Perhaps we have been forgotten, we have never been introduced, or humans have been so busy with so much these days (fear, money, power, etc.) that they have lost sight of why they are here in the first place: to learn how to live in duality. And I'm not talking about the day-to-day hustle and bustle of your world. I'm talking about breathing the air and feeling the vibrations of not only the world but also the universe. If you have picked this up and read it thus far, you have likely begun this wider understanding of the universe. Or perhaps you are quite far in your journey, and with your elevated frequency, you're interested in reading what the energies in this book have to offer you. Wherever you are in your understanding of the universe as a human, welcome. This collection of energies will provide you with the tools to assuage any fear(s) you may have regarding the concept of death and allow you to begin living. So let's begin.

Why am I narrating this book or guide? The answer is very simple: Because I asked. Ha, ha! Does it surprise you to know that I have an excellent sense of humor? At least in my estimation I do. Now, the reason that I wanted to narrate this guide and not be connected to one of the numbers is a different issue. The exact answer to that is a bit complicated. It will be understood by the time that you get to the end of this guide. However, what I will tell you now is that there is a combination of reasons. While there are many energies who are qualified to narrate (collectives are also qualified), it was decided that I should narrate. Many humans hear my name and regard me as quite knowledgeable on this subject. But then energies such as myself are also not spoken of as often as we were centuries ago. So when you hear my name, there are not as many preconceived notions as there are if I were to say the name Jesus or Mary. I am free to introduce myself without you having made certain judgments about what I should or should not say.

Let's begin this journey with a discussion about consciousness. Have you ever connected with your own higher consciousness? Some might call this your higher self. Let me explain what I mean when I say your higher self. I use this term to describe your form of consciousness that is unionized with the divine. Your higher self is unencumbered by ego and therefore, unencumbered by fear. Connecting to your higher self is part of the process that will take you to meet your transmutation guide or guides. Some readers already understand this concept and need to think only of their higher self to connect. Because there are those who have not yet consciously met their higher selves, I will give you a method to connect (and I am quite excited to assist).

I, as the narrator, will be leading the discussion with each of these energies. Sometimes I will be prompting them with questions and guiding them through this process with you. Other times, the guide will lead the entire discussion. However, please note that each of them takes this process seriously. You will essentially be creating a contract with one or more of these energies. You will form a relationship with one or more of them, and they will most certainly abide by the terms of the contract.

To start, I have created a contract for you to review and complete before beginning. I am able to do this because the transcriptionist for this book is an attorney. Therefore, I am able to access her breadth of knowledge on this topic. Do not enter the information and sign it until you are ready to do so.

I, _____ (print name) hereby enter into the following contract on _____ (date) with Anubis. I do this freely and without reservation. The said parties, for the consideration hereafter mentioned, agree to the following terms.

I hereby give to Anubis my permission to work with me and my higher self and to guide me in my preparation for transmutation. I give Anubis the authority to take any corrective measures he deems appropriate for purposes of the guide I choose to lead me into transmutation.

I give Anubis my permission to energetically increase my vibration through my crown chakra, my third-eye chakra, and my pineal gland. This energy transfer binds Anubis to me and me to Anubis. Any additional energetic transfer shall require a different contract between myself and Anubis.

This agreement may be canceled by burning the paper on which it has been signed.

I understand that this contract represents a profound act of surrender to and trust in higher spiritual guidance.

Signature: _____

Date: _____

As you saw, this contract requires me to give an energy transfer to you. You may do this by stating the following sentence three times: "In my journey to connect with my higher self, I seek the assistance of Anubis." Now, please say the following sentence three times: "Before I begin to connect with my higher self, Anubis, please ensure that each of my chakras are open and turning clockwise." Then just breathe in and out through your nose three times. When you breathe out, allow it to sound like Darth Vader's breathing. Next, while you breathe in, count to six. Hold it for six counts and then breathe out for six counts. Do this same process but breathe in for seven, hold for seven, and breathe out for seven. Do the same with eight. Breathe in for eight, hold for eight, and then breathe out for eight. Do you feel the energy running through your crown and third-eye chakras? Close your eyes. What do you see forming in the shadows? Perhaps it is an eye, a dog, or a symbol? Whatever you see, that is what you will think of or focus on whenever you try to contact me.

Choosing your guide or guides comes next. There are eleven guides. Each number (one, two, three, etc.) carries a specific vibrational frequency. When combined with a specific guide, the frequency changes. It becomes a combination of energy emanating from the particular number and the energy emanating from the particular guide. If you wish, you may read through the particular guides first and perhaps choose one whom you already have an interest in. You may also read this entire book without asking any particular guide to assist you with your transmutation journey and choose one or more guides after becoming familiar with each. You may also ask me to assist you in choosing your guide.

If you would like my assistance, let's begin. As humans, you each have a unique frequency or vibration. That frequency or vibration may increase or decrease. For example, if you meditate daily and connect with other frequencies or vibrations, you are increasing your frequency or vibration. Things like fear, hatred, and jealousy decrease your vibration. Like humans, certain numbers carry certain vibrations. Now, close your eyes and focus on the energy frequency or the symbol or image that you saw during my earlier energy transmission to you. Now, breathe in and out very slowly. With your mind's eye, find the numbers one through eleven. Set them up in the manner that you feel best represents the sequence. (Perhaps the numbers are lined up numerically, in a circle, or in different locations throughout space.) Are they different colors? Are some bold and some italicized? Do some have a certain sound connected to them? Now, ask me to connect with your energy. Take a minute to feel my energy and get used to it. This may take seconds or it may take a few minutes. Just breathe in and out and concentrate on the connection between you and me. Next, concentrate on picking one of the numbers. Please know that there is no wrong answer here. If you do not see any number that jumps out at you, just continue breathing until one does. You may connect with more than one number. You may start by going straight to that number/energy below and who is connected to that number. You may also start at the beginning of the list below, read through each of the energies, and see which one (or two or three) that you connect with the most.

When you move on to the particular guide, please let me know that you are ready to move on. I will continue with you on your journey for as long as you like. Additionally, I will have specific messages for you at the close of this book. I thank you for this opportunity.

Before beginning, I want to give you a quick note. I am a sort of gatekeeper for this book. All the energies are from the light; I have made sure of that. I also keep out any potential negative energies while the transcriptionist is channeling. I say this because some people will look at certain energies and have an immediate reaction or thought that says some are not from the light. But they are. Here is a quick summation of the participants.

ARCHANGEL URIEL

Archangel Uriel is often a guardian of those who have the faith to seek out and find the truth and the wisdom that they bring. They are there to assist you on your journey toward a closer relationship with the divine or in hearing and receiving divine messages and presences. Archangel Uriel places high importance on service since they understands that we cannot just know the divine message on our own. When it comes to their personal, professional, and spiritual truths, Uriel aims to get to the bottom of everything. There are times when the truth scares us. For this reason alone, Uriel may be considered terrifying. They may show up when you least expect it or are least prepared to receive the truth. Uriel is associated with the number one. If you picked this number, you are inquisitive. Number one is a sign of a new beginning because it is the initial number. It is related to ambition, leadership, independence, and positivity. You may have some fear of change, but with this number and Archangel Uriel's help, you will get over the fear of transmutation. Have faith in yourself and your gut feelings. Uriel's name means the light of God, which signifies nothing less than illuminating your path. When it comes to finding your truth, Archangel Uriel will shine a light on anything that might be hindering your progress.

XIA

She is high priestess in the galactic federation. As a high priestess, she performs sacred rights and teaches others those sacred rights. She symbolizes divine illumination, inner enlightenment, and wisdom from the divine. She is connected to water. She is associated with the qualities of emotion and intuition. She is part of the white *zeta reticuli* race. Zeta Reticuli is a white-to-yellow star, which is located in the constellation of Reticulum. Two is associated with the colors white and purple and the scent of vanilla. Two is a symbol of balance, prosperity, teamwork, peace, and harmony. People who choose this number are likely able to shift their perspectives and rethink their beliefs. They are willing to accept and adapt to change. Known as the peacemaker, two is almost always gentle, tactful, diplomatic, forgiving, and nonconfrontational. However, the shape of the number two gives us a clue to its resilience and ability to survive. As if bowing in servitude, this symbol could easily be perceived as weak and powerless. But when the humble number two is under attack and even burdened by a crushing weight, its flexible nature allows it to bounce back quickly. Twos understand the underlying motivation that drives the people around them. The ability to understand others helps them navigate divergent opinions and ideas, gives a little here, and takes a little there. Many psychotherapists who are skilled at reading human nature have a strong number two in their charts. Patient and unassuming, twos don't always get the recognition they deserve. But they tend to hold a special place in the hearts and minds of those who know them. The number two is recognized for its grace, sophistication, style, and taste in art and music. Dancers often carry this number due to its inherent sense of rhythm. In social environments, twos are good conversationalists and have witty, self-depreciating senses of humor (never slapstick or juvenile, as they are too sophisticated for that).

THE MORRIGAN AND CROW MAGICK

The Morrigan, the Celtic goddess of magick, is associated with witchcraft, protection, war, fate, and foretelling death or victory in battle. She is a shape-shifter and often takes the form of a crow or a raven. She is a triple goddess and is often described as a trio of sisters called the three Morrigan. These three sisters could take the form of a single goddess. In many sources, Badb, Macha, and Nemain are named as The Morrigan; although sometimes it is given as Badb, Macha, and Dannan/Danu (or Anand/Anu). The crow is associated with foresight, vision, wit, selflessness, and occasional mischief. The crow spirit guide helps you not to fear change. Transmutation may seem difficult, so the crow steps in to support your effort with greater insights. The crow gives your spirit the gift of watchfulness, both physical and psychic and as a result, the ability to protect those you love. Working with the crow's energy and medicine, you can begin to see how energies mix, mingle, and transform on an alchemical level.

The number three is closely linked to feelings of hope and optimism. It is a representation of wisdom and balance. If you have picked number three, you are likely to be very self-assured. You like to maintain balance in your life. The concept of a human being is embodied in the number three. Body, spirit, and mind are all represented by it. And there are three basic elements that make up the Earth's composition: water, heaven, and sky.

KALI

She is the Hindu goddess of time, change, creation, destruction, and power. She embodies *shakti* (feminine energy). Her symbols are flowers, dancing, iron, swords, peacock feathers, and honey. Her fragrances are jasmine, rose, and sandalwood. The number four is associated with her. It represents self-expression, self-fulfillment, maturity and stability of mind. It is associated with spiritual enlightenment and a strong will. A natural cycle begins after four seasons, making a perfect circle. The number four denotes a state of completion and contentment. The number four is associated with the creation of the world; thus, Kali's path and relationship with you will be a creative one. A four is adequately equipped for work because of their ability to focus on the details and the steps required to reach specific goals. Those of you who chose this number are likely to be conscientious. You may also be blunt when asked for opinions regarding the execution of any project or the feasibility of a new project. You see the details and respond according to how you perceive things. Four represents a composition containing the ideas of focus, foundation, conscientiousness, method, and pragmatism.

APHRODITE

She is the Greek goddess of sexual love and beauty. She is known as the goddess of love and fertility. Her belt (cestus) had the power to cause others to fall in love with the wearer. Her symbols are doves, pomegranates, swans, and myrtles. Her flower is the red anemone. The number five represents the perfection of the five senses and the nuptial number of love and union. The number five represents spiritual growth and self-confidence. The five-pointed star was a symbol for Aphrodite's Roman counterpart, Venus. A knot in the shape of a five-pointed star is referred to in England as a lover's knot. The number is connected with a great deal of vitality, adaptability, and independence. People who have picked this number are likely to be emotional and to have a pure and clean heart. They have a strong sense of loyalty, and they would never betray a relationship. The focus here will be on the heart chakra.

GUAN YIN, GUAN YIM, KUAN YIM, KWAN IM, KUAN YIN, OR KUAN-SHI YIN

These mean "observing the sounds (or cries) of the (human) world." She is the goddess of compassion, mercy, and kindness. In Sanskrit, she's knowns as Padma Pani, meaning "born of the lotus." The lotus symbolizes purity, peace, and harmony. She is usually depicted as wearing a white robe (symbolizing purity) and necklaces of Indian and Chinese royalty. In her right hand, she holds a water jar. As the sacred vase, the water jar is also one of the eight Buddhist symbols of good fortune. The jar contains pure water, the divine nectar of life, compassion, and wisdom. In her left hand, she holds a willow branch, which she uses to sprinkle the divine nectar of life on the devotees to bless them with physical and spiritual peace. The willow branch is also a symbol of being able to bend (or adapt) but not break. The willow is also used in shamanistic rituals. It has medicinal purposes as well. Kuan Yin symbolizes kindness, love, compassion, pity, empathy, concern, and sometimes solicitude. These are not only exhibited emotions, but she symbolizes the divine love and energy that comes from enlightenment. She is the epitome of love. She is also associated with vegetarianism, as she signifies the values of purity, compassion, and mercy. Six is her number.

The Pythagoreans acknowledged the number six to be the first perfect number. In mathematics, a perfect number is when all the number's divisors (excluding the number itself) are added, and the sum equals the number itself (1+2+3=6). In addition, when including the number itself and dividing by two, the result is the number itself (1+2+3+6) /2 = 6. Perfect numbers are rare. The ancient Greeks recognized four perfect numbers: 6, 28, 496, and 8,128. Throughout history, perfect numbers have fascinated mathematicians.

The number six is the embodiment of the heart. It represents unconditional love and the ability to support, nurture, and heal. It is a powerful force of compassion and empathy. Its warm light is a beacon of hope. Its role is to use its heart and soul to be of service to others. When a shoulder is needed to lean on, those people who have picked the number six will likely be the first to arrive, equipped with a kind, soft presence and heartfelt advice. Sixes do not simply wait to speak; they truly listen and seek to understand so that they may direct their compassion and healing to where it is needed most. If you have chosen six, you likely have a deep sense of compassion, and you are loving, caring, and selfless. You are likely very empathetic, and you may have constructed a wall around yourself to stay protected.

MIMIR

In Norse mythology, the giant Mimir (or Mim) was considered the wisest member of the group of gods known as the Aesir. He served as the guardian of Mimisbrunnr, the well of knowledge located at the base of the world tree Yggdrasill. During the war between the Aesir and another group of gods called the Vanir, the Vanir took Mimir and a companion named Hoenir as hostages. Hoenir was treated as a chieftain by the Vanir, but without Mim, Hoenir could not speak well. The Vanir felt cheated, cut off Mim's head, and sent it back to Odin, the father of the gods, who kept it alive in a shrine near the base of Yggdrasill. The well of knowledge sprang from the spot where Mim's head was kept.

Seeking wisdom, Odin rode to the well to drink its water. However, Mim allowed him to do so only after Odin left one of his eyes in the well. From then on when Odin wished to learn secrets from the well, he asked questions of Mim's head, which gave him the answers. Although you will not need to sacrifice an eye in exchange for Mim's knowledge and guidance, he does ask that you make a gift to him (like purchasing a book about him or a figurine). Mim is associated with wisdom and the pursuit of knowledge. He is the number seven. Seven is the number of perfection, security, safety, and rest. Seven contains the numbers three (the heavens and soul) and four (the Earth and body). Seven circles form the symbol called the Seed of Life (see Chapter Five for a greater explanation of a picture of the Seed of Life). The Seed of Life symbolizes the six days of creation. The central circle symbolizes the day of rest. The number seven is both deep and wise. It is not satisfied with simple explanations and surface-level information—this is frivolous stuff. It knows that the real gold is buried deeper. It won't stop until it finds it. Then it'll keep digging for more. If you picked number seven, it is likely in your personality to ask questions, research, listen, and sense things. Sevens take a more intellectual approach to life than an emotional one. It is an analytical number, which enjoys gathering and filtering through information to find answers. Still, it has a more powerful intuition than you might expect, which it uses as a guide. This combination of conscious and subconscious thinking allows the mind of a seven to shine a light into the very deepest realms to access hidden truths.

HECATE OR HEKATE AND THE WITCH

This is the only category that will have two separate energies or forces. Hekate is a goddess in ancient Greek religion and mythology. She was most often shown holding a pair of torches, a key, and snakes and accompanied by dogs. She is known as a triple goddess (like The Morrigan) and is associated with crossroads, magick, witchcraft, the Moon, knowledge of herbs and poisonous plants, graves, ghosts, necromancy, and sorcery. She is one of the few who walks in both the light and the dark. Because she was one of the deities worshipped by The Witch, she is included within this number (and book). To invoke Hekate, you must use caution. Once you have invoked her, you will be bound to her and her energy.

The Witch is a fierce, primordial energy. If you have chosen this number, you have likely spent some time with the Witch (or one of her avatars) in a past life. The pupils of her eyes are yellow, and the surrounding irises are red. Her original coven, which was formed in Africa, was called the Komati. Facing prejudice and mistreatment, the Komati coven traveled from Africa to India, where they settled. This coven was made up of only women. Some were healers, some were mediums, and all were fierce. The coven had four wolves, all of whom traveled with them to India. The Witch assisted the Komati with transcribing some of what would later be called the Book of the Dead. Included in the Komati's transcribing was a chapter on transmutation. The Witch is associated with the scent of sandalwood. She is also associated with the wolf. The wolf spirit carries a message of discipline and order. Like howling at the moon and greeting pack members upon their return, wolf spirits maintain many rituals. The structure and order of the animal pack has great meaning and ensures security and purpose for all of its members. Sometimes the wolf calls on us to become the lone wolf, who breaks away from the pack to discover the sacred self. During times of aloneness, you rediscover your dreams and passions. You also start uncovering the true self and voice that howls at the moon with abandon.

Those who choose the number eight are achievers, and they measure life by the goals they reach. You have a good business sense, a powerful presence, and a strong drive for success. Eight is also a symbol of balance; you can see it in its symmetrical shape. For every blessing it receives, it sends one back out to the universe. When things are balanced, eights feel stable, controlled, and supported, which is the most productive environment for eights to work in. When rotated ninety degrees, an eight becomes the infinity symbol, which is significant here because it means that you have made a previous contract with The Witch. And The Witch is infinitely loyal. In a spiritual sense, the number eight is all about giving back. It realizes that its successes are not its alone. It will intentionally recognize and appreciate any help it has received. It balances achievement with gratitude, which can then be rebalanced with more achievement. It's a cycle of success that eight continuously manifests.

QUETZALCOATL

He is the Aztec feathered, serpent God. He was the god of winds and rain and the creator of the world and humanity. He was considered the patron god of priests and merchants, as well as the god of learning, science, agriculture, crafts, and the arts. He also invented the calendar, was identified with the morning star Venus, and was associated with opossums. He even discovered corn (maize) with the help of a giant red ant, which led him to a mountain packed full of grain and seeds. His emblem is a half conch, the symbol of creation. He is number nine. Number nine represents completion. It is the last of the single-digit numbers and the highest in value. It represents the culmination of wisdom and experience, as it represents endings and new beginnings. The number nine has a lot of power because it's closely associated with spiritual awakening. It is a symbol of patience, tranquility, faith, and love. Personalities with this number are likely to be tolerant, stable, and dependable. They are also known for their high levels of energy, competitiveness, and creativity. Most nines are people who enjoy helping others and who have based their careers on love instead of money.

ENKI

Among the many other gods worshiped by the Mesopotamians, some of the most important were the Anunnaki or the seven gods who were the most powerful: Enki, Enlil, Ninhursag, An, Inanna, Utu, and Nanna. The Anunnaki are believed to be immortal ancient gods that inhabited the Earth during the Sumerian time in Mesopotamia. The Sumerian civilization developed on the Persian Gulf, growing to strength at around 4,000–3,000 BC. The ancient Sumerians were the first recorded civilization of humankind. They were highly advanced in currency, astronomy, and farming. Enki, later known as Ea by the Akkadians and Babylonians, was the Sumerian deity of wisdom, intelligence, tricks and magic, fresh water, healing, creation, and fertility. Originally, he was worshiped as the patron god of Eridu, which the Sumerians considered to be the first city created when the world began. According to myth, Enki gave birth to the Tigris and Euphrates rivers. They came from the streams of water flowing off his body. Enki's waters are considered to be life-giving. His symbols are the goat and the fish, both of which symbolize fertility. The turtle is also associated with Enki. The Sumerian *En* translates roughly into lord, and *ki* means Earth. Thus, the commonly accepted meaning of his name is Lord of the Earth. Enki's other name is Ea. In Sumerian, when the two syllables E and A are put together, it means Lord of Water. He is number ten. Number ten symbolizes the completion of a cycle. It is the number of heaven, the world, and universal creation. Ten is the very first number that needs a separate part. Number ten was the holiest according to the Pythagoreans. Pythagoras believed that number ten represented the universe and the sum of human knowledge. Pythagoreans (his followers) believed this to be the holiest of numbers and took their oaths by swearing on the symbol of the number ten. The digits one and zero indicate the masculine and feminine principles together. Ten indicates an independent person with enormous potential. This number helps in bringing projects to completion. The number ten is comfortable with being alone (like the number one), and it recognizes the need for individualism while being part of the whole—as the number zero is concerned with inclusion. The essence of number one is an inversion of the essence of number zero. Number one steps away from a oneness or wholeness with everything and transmits a different vibration from the zero (or any other number for that matter). A divine number, ten means a return to unity and the fusion of being and nonbeing. The number ten denotes the completion of a cycle, making tens very skilled at whatever they choose to do. And they do so on their own terms.

PAPA LEGBA

In Haitian Vodou and New Orleans Voodoo, Papa Legba is the intermediary between the *loa* (*lwa*) and humanity. He stands at a spiritual crossroads and grants or denies permission to speak with the spirits of Guinee. He is believed to speak all human languages. He is always the first and the last spirit invoked in any ceremony because his permission is needed for any communication between mortals and the loa. He opens and closes the doorway to the spirit world. Papa Legba is a master linguist, trickster, warrior, and the personal messenger of destiny. He has the power to remove obstacles, and he provides opportunities. His colors are red and black. Some of his favorite things, which can be used as offerings, include candy, cigars, rum, and tobacco. He also loves palm oil. He would like to say a few words before his chapter begins.

"I may be thought of as someone fierce, but I also have a softer side. We all do. For example, Kali is thought of as a fierce energy. But does she not have a softer side? The inverse is also true. Aphrodite is thought of as a softer energy. But she also has a fierce side. Is not loving fiercely still ferocious? So you see, while I might have a formidable reputation, the contact I will have with you through this journey is a softer one. While I am sometimes associated with the number three, I step aside for The Morrigan (or Crow Magick) to claim that number. For the purpose of this guidance, I will claim number eleven."

Number eleven is associated with qualities such as initiative, optimism, and a positive outlook on life. Self-expression and originality are also associated with this number. People who have chosen the number eleven are likely greatest at being philosophers, artists, musicians, teachers, and performers. Artistic or spiritual brilliance may be found in any occupation. The vibrational frequency of number eleven is one of balance. It also depicts the equality of men and women. The number eleven is associated with spiritual awakening. This mystical number is said to offer insight, higher energy, inspiration, and creativity. Eleven is considered to be the gateway to enlightenment and transformation through intuition and balance. If you have chosen this number, you are likely a deep thinker. You also must be very focused on a specific goal; otherwise, you may develop fear and anxiety, which can sometimes be overwhelming. Eleven presents itself to people who appear to be psychically connected.

CHAPTER 1

ARCHANGEL URIEL

Hello, my beloved. I am the archangel Uriel. I recognize some readers are already in doubt. And that is wonderful because in your world of duality, without doubt, there is no certainty. I am here to give you the truth and certainty that there is so much more to experience after death. I require no contract or profession on your part. For you see, I am pure light and consciousness. I am also androgynous. All angels are. You see, we have never lived in human form. Those who are labeled as "transgendered" may find that for purposes of this book, I connect to them the most. You see, they have already had an understanding of transmutation while still in human form. They have an understanding of what it is like to be both male and female. While that is still different from being androgynous, it is the closest to me energetically.

My gift to you is that of consciousness. Being conscious (being present) in this world is important. Learning to be present is the first step in the journey of preparing for transmutation. Also, I find the irony in learning how to be present in this moment is the best way to prepare for the future. Ha, ha! But this is true. As humans, many of you have developed so much stress, anxiety, and worry over future events, likely because of past events that have transpired. This creates an environment in which you are almost always looking behind you or too far in the future to know whether these worries or stresses are even within the realm of probabilities. This in turn, lessens your ability to be happy and present within your life.

Let me ask you this: Why do you worry about something that has already passed? It seems like your answer is because you worry that it will happen again. But why worry *now* about something that may not ever come to pass? Your life and the events that have transpired have led you here. And here is an astounding place to be. You have both spirit and body. Would it surprise you to know that there are so many beings who have only spirits? Think about what not being able to enjoy food or drink or to hold your loved ones would be like. Being joyous about who and what you are right now is an important first step in transmuting from the combination of body and spirit into just spirit.

So start by tapping your right index finger on your third eye three times (located in the middle of your forehead). Say the phrase, "Archangel Uriel, help me to be present." Then tap three times and repeat that phrase. Do this one more time (or however many times you feel you should). When you feel like you are not being present, do this exercise. It is so simple. Sometimes all you need is that little push to get started seeing things as simply as they really are.

The human brain seems to complicate certain things. I understand that sometimes there is the question if God made everything, what made God? The answer is so simple. God has always been. Humans love to believe that time is linear. It is not. It is circular. Just as a circle has no end or beginning, neither does God. Can you believe that you died before— more than once? Sometimes your death has been traumatic. Sometimes it has been a peaceful passing. Sometimes your death has come to you on a different planet, plane, or dimension. Can you believe that because time is a circle, you are leading lives that intertwine and intersect with the one you are living right now? It is quite a concept to take in. Perhaps it might be too much to take in for some. But for those of you who embrace this concept, you will start living in the present so much sooner.

So there are those of you who are wondering about fate. Are some events fate? Yes. But not all events are fated to happen. You see, there are certain contracts that you have made with others before coming to Earth. Some of those contracts are with individuals who perhaps feel indebted to you. Some contracts are with others who would like to have the chance to pay back their karmic debts. For example, perhaps you married someone who mistreated you in a previous life. Perhaps there is a contract between you two, and this person would like the chance to make up for his or her past misdeeds. That is the part that is fated. However, whether this person "karmically" repairs what has been broken (i.e., treats you better) is not fated. This is where free will enters into the picture. Perhaps this person is just as mean to you in this lifetime as he or she was in the past. Then the question for you is in the next lifetime—should you choose to come back—will you allow this person to fix his or her karma?

These types of contracts are made all the time between and among souls. You have a contract with your spirit guides. You may have been a guide to them in a past life. Your parent in this lifetime may have been your child in a past lifetime. You do not always keep the same souls within your life circle, but sometimes there are very many cross references.

This brings me to what we are here to do—understand how to begin preparing for transmutation. For me, being present is the best way to begin because it will bring you so much more joy on a day-to-day basis. And when you do the exercise that I previously mentioned, you will be able to call on me. I will assist you in those times when you wish to be present, but you are not able to get there without some assistance.

Once you have practiced being present, the next step will be an energy transfer. Although you do not need to have had Anubis's energy transfer to receive this energy transfer, it is more beneficial to your frequency or vibration to have both. Also, please note that I recommend that you request this energy transfer before a time of rest—perhaps before you fall asleep or before meditation. You will receive the greatest benefit if this occurs at a time when you are relaxed, and your body is in a state where it welcomes this new energy.

My energy transfer will come through your third eye. As you may note, the exercise I just explained consists of tapping your third eye. All communication with me will occur through your third eye. This energy transfer will enable you to contact me quickly and to sense my energy and/or frequency. To get this energy transfer, please say the following three times: "Archangel Uriel, please connect with me through my third eye." Everyone will feel this energy transfer differently. Please pay close attention to what you see after making the statement three times. I recommend keeping your eyes closed because this will help you use your third eye to reach out to me. Do you see a symbol or a color? Do you hear a specific song playing? Whatever you see or hear will be our starting point for purposes of your being able to call out to me and then recognize my energy.

Now I know there is at least one person who has the following question: What if more than one person needs me at the same time? This will likely happen with more energies than just me. I will try to explain this in terms that the human mind is able to understand. There are two components at work here. First, remember when I stated that time is not linear but circular? Well, working with time is not an issue when you understand its circular nature. Second, being in spirit form makes it even easier to be in more than one place at the same time. I suppose you could say that knowing how to work with time could be bending time. But again, time is not only circular. It works very differently in different planes and dimensions (i.e., how quickly or slowly it passes). I am able to extend my spirit to all who need my assistance when my assistance is needed.

I would now like to explain a bit about chakras—specifically, your third-eye chakra. In Sanskrit, the word *chakra* means disk or wheel and refers to the energy centers of your body. These wheels or disks of spinning energy correspond to certain nerve bundles and major organs. To function at their best, your chakras need to stay open or balanced. If they get blocked, you may experience physical or emotional symptoms related to a particular chakra. The seven main chakras run along your spine. They start at the root or base of your spine and extend to the crown of your head. The chakras most often referred to are the seven main ones.

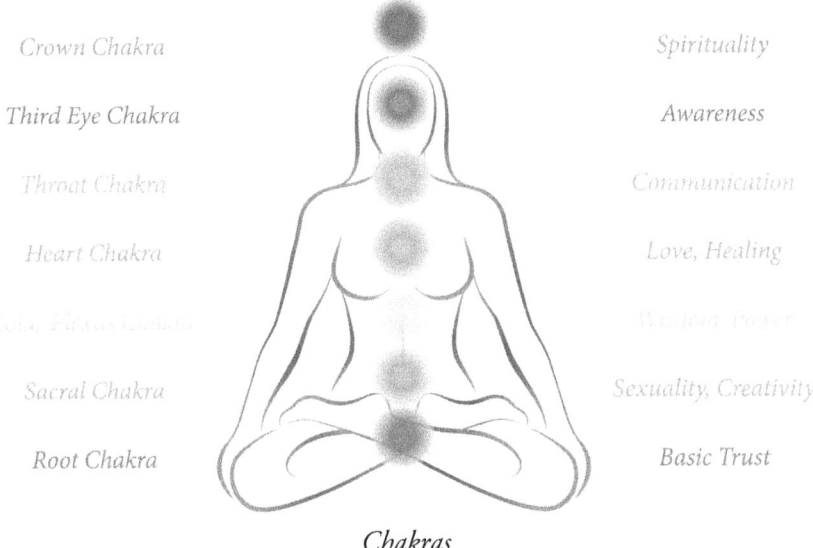

Crown Chakra		Spirituality
Third Eye Chakra		Awareness
Throat Chakra		Communication
Heart Chakra		Love, Healing
Solar Plexus Chakra		Wisdom, Power
Sacral Chakra		Sexuality, Creativity
Root Chakra		Basic Trust

Chakras

The third-eye chakra is your sixth chakra. It is located on your forehead between your eyebrows. It is the center of intuition and foresight. The most common Sanskrit name for the third-eye chakra is *ajna*, which means command and perceiving. This chakra is related to the supreme element, which is the combination of all the elements in their pure forms. The third-eye chakra is most commonly represented with the color purple or bluish purple. The auric color of the third-eye chakra's energy can also be seen as translucent purple or bluish white. You can thank this chakra for a strong gut instinct. That's because the third eye is responsible for intuition. It's also linked to imagination.

I know that some readers may be overwhelmed right now. Some readers may not have known that spirituality would have some crossovers with the human body. There is so much that must work in union to be able to achieve enlightenment. But with each step you take up that ladder, the easier transmutation will become. For some, this guide or book will be your first step. For others, this will only supplement what you already know. Either way, putting in the work (whether it's step one or one thousand) is what will make the transmutation process easier.

Think of your chakras (in particular, your third-eye chakra) like a muscle. If you cannot use your muscles for a while, and you are bedridden, what happens to them? They atrophy. If you work out daily and build your muscles with certain exercises, they become stronger. The more you reach out with your third-eye chakra and connect with me, the easier it will become. The easier it becomes, the easier transmutation will become.

Before we really get into the topic of death and transmutation, let's first talk about life. I have already explained that being present is very important. Happiness is important. Did you know that happiness is a choice? Some people will read that and think, *What? That's ridiculous!* But I ask that you think about this for a minute. Let's take the situation of a close friend or family member passing on. Of course, you will miss this person's physical being. That person is no longer around to laugh with, hug, or talk to. But rather than dwelling on those aspects, why not dwell on the times when you laughed with, hugged, or kissed this person? I understand there is a period when you must grieve. I understand this is an important step for humans to process another human's passing. But my point is that once you have appropriately grieved, rejoice in the happiness that you shared together. Know that when these humans passed on, they remembered that happiness and took it with them as they transformed.

Practice being happy. Being happy upon passing makes the transmutation process much easier. Consider this a type of homework. Before going to bed, think about the happiness you felt during the day. Think about what it was like to feel connected to your friend or family member. (I am including pets as family members.) What made you thankful? Did you feel loved? Did you make someone else feel loved? Building on these feelings assists with enlightenment. Perhaps you are thinking, *I did not have anything happen today to make me feel joyful.* Perhaps that is true. Then your homework is to do something that makes you feel joyful every day.

Letting go takes practice. What do I mean by letting go? I mean letting go of anger, impatience, jealousy, doubt, anxiety, stress, or anything that lowers your frequency or vibration. Practicing letting go will assist you with transmutation because letting go is one of the main issues that people have in not being able to cross over. Guilt plays a very large factor in this. Sometimes people feel guilty for not conveying a certain message of love to another person. They feel guilty for leaving someone behind. Perhaps they feel guilty for sins that they believe they have committed. Please understand guilt is a human feeling. During transmutation, once you have reached a certain point in the process, and as you are crossing over, you will not feel this way. So practicing letting go will assist you with eventually transmuting your consciousness from your human form into the next realm or dimension.

Well now, some of you are thinking, *That's easy for you, Archangel Uriel. You're an angel. You don't know what it's like to feel extreme guilt.* But again, perhaps that guilt is what you needed out of your human experience. You have been guided to read my explanation about how to transmute your consciousness. So perhaps it is time to let go of that guilt. Someone may read this and think, *Oh, great! I should do whatever I want now and not feel guilt!* That is not what I'm saying. Anyone (human or otherwise) with half a brain would know that is not what I'm saying. It is for you to determine how to deal with your guilt in order to let go of it. Perhaps you owe someone an apology. Or perhaps you just need to apologize to yourself. If you feel like you should apologize to someone who has already crossed over, tell that person through your third eye that you apologize. He or she will hear you. That, I promise.

If you would like some help with letting go, I have an exercise for you. Focus on your third eye. Think about what you felt during my energy transmission. You may ask me to help you with this if you like. Think about an event or a time when you felt guilty, jealous, or impatient. Bring those thoughts to your third eye. Feel the emotions collecting into a whirlpool. This whirlpool may be made of whatever you wish. Perhaps it is water, fire, or blood. There is no incorrect material. Keep collecting those thoughts and emotions into your third eye. Think about that event or time coming into your third eye through your body and the energy around your body. Call on me to place my hand on your third eye and collect those thoughts and emotions. Do you feel yourself becoming lighter? Do you feel your vibration increasing? Is there a particular song that you hear or vision that you get? Continue with this exercise as many times as you wish. I understand that with humans, just because you let go of a negative thought this one time does not mean that you will not think about that event again. It just means that all the negative emotions connected to that event up until now have been released. If you continue to dwell on that experience, those emotions will collect again. One way you can keep from thinking about that negative event is to be present. If you need help with being present, continue to practice the exercise described above. I understand that this is a difficult practice for humans. Many of you feel guilt, sadness, etc. very often. It is within your makeup to think about experiences and then build on them. But when an experience is no longer benefiting you, letting go of those thoughts makes room for you to create and build other experiences to think about. Making it a practice to think about positive experiences will increase your vibration. Increasing your vibration will make it easier for your consciousness to transmute.

What is consciousness? Perhaps some would prefer that I call this your soul. That word was created by a human. It does not encapsulate everything that consciousness really is. So I prefer not to use that word. Are you surprised? If you are, it might be because you have grouped me into a very specific type of religious belief. Some of the writings within that religious belief are beneficial to humans and some are not. As we all know, those writings were made by men. Men made archangels to look like men. As I stated earlier, I am neither man nor woman. No archangels are. We are androgynous. I understand the human need to classify and categorize. But have you not thought it odd that we are all male? It does make me laugh to think that there are some humans who believe that heaven is made up of all men. No women are allowed! Ha, ha, ha! I cannot reiterate how silly that is. If you are reading this, you are a human who is reading this and understanding that there is so much more to consciousness than the stories in books that men have written. There are countless dimensions and planes. Your consciousness takes part in creation more than you know. Finish this statement: "If I could create, I would create _____." Your word in that statement indicates where your vibrational frequency is at right now. If you answered that you would create wealth for yourself, the reasoning behind that is important. For example, if you want to create wealth for yourself so that you can open a large dog shelter to help homeless animals, it's an indication that you are working toward creating a better world. If you want to create wealth for yourself so that you can do whatever you want (i.e., you just want to be lazy), I think you do not need me to finish that thought.

A higher vibrational frequency is important because the higher your vibrational frequency, the higher energy you attract. If your vibrational frequency is low (due to something like frequent alcohol consumption), you will attract others with that same lower frequency. You will also attract nonhuman energy at that frequency (or even lower). Increasing your vibrational frequency takes work. But that is why some of you are on Earth—not only to learn how to increase your own vibrational frequency but also to help others increase their vibrational frequencies.

If you chose number one, you were attracted not only to that number's frequency but also to my frequency combined with that number. The number one is the beginning of a journey. The number zero is a balancing number. There isn't anything on either side—nothing positive or negative but only zero. The number one indicates that first step toward something positive. The number one also indicates being first in line or winning first place. Are you just starting this journey toward transmutation or the first to cross the finish line because this is your final step of preparation? You see how it could indicate both thoughts at the same time?

My frequency combined with the number one is 528 hertz. What does this signify? It is the love frequency and is thought to resonate at the core of everything. It connects our hearts, our spiritual natures, and the divine harmony. The 528-hertz frequency is a sensational tone, which has been used since ancient civilizations to manifest miracles, bring blessings, and harness healing properties. This frequency brings transformation and an increased amount of love energy, clarity of mind, awareness, activated creativity, and inner peace. It also has the ability to activate your imagination, intention, and intuition so that they operate for your highest and best purpose. You have the internet, so you can google 528-hertz frequency and listen to it. Listening to it while going through some of the exercises I have given in this chapter is preferable. You will be able to connect with me, your consciousness, and the universe much quicker while listening to this frequency (with practice).

You may ask yourself, *What does it feel like to connect with the universe?* It feels different for everyone. But the overall feeling is one of harmony and peace. When you are able to expand your consciousness, which you may do on this plane, you may recognize why people decide not to eat meat or to help those who are less fortunate or in an unjust situation. Giving another human even the smallest bit of hope helps to increase your frequency. I am not saying that eating meat lowers your frequency. I am just explaining that when your consciousness expands, and you are able to connect with an animal, you will be able to recognize that the way in which most of society consumes meat (i.e., slaughtering millions of animals and throwing away much of the meat) is careless.

I understand that these concepts may be coming at some people a bit too fast to understand. Do not worry. You may need to read this more than once. You may ask that I conduct the energy transfer more than once. I will continue to attempt to raise your frequency as many times as you ask me to. The important thing for you to know is that your frequency will not increase when you are consuming alcohol. I am not trying to discourage anyone from living the way that they want to. I am just giving you the facts. You may take them or leave them.

The goal for you is to be able to expand your consciousness while you are on this Earth. Doing so will make transmutation much easier. As everything in life, expanding your consciousness takes much time and dedication. But it can be done. One potential path is meditation and/or yoga. I understand that meditation and yoga are not preferable to everyone. You may also expand your consciousness in the dream state. To expand your consciousness in the dream state, before going to sleep, reach out to me using your third eye. Say the following three times: "Archangel Uriel, come to me in the dream state and help to expand my consciousness in preparation for transmutation." I recommend keeping a journal of what you dream about. Although some of your dreams may not seem to be expanding your consciousness, they are. And some dreams you will not remember. But the more you do this before falling asleep, the easier it will be to recall your dreams. Eventually, you will feel like you have traveled in your dreams. When you have a dream such as this, you will know. It will take you a minute or two to become fully conscious after waking up. You may hear a loud "boom" upon waking. This is your consciousness reentering your body. For some, being able to travel with your consciousness will happen quickly. For others, it may take some time. But just know that as long as you state the sentence given above, I will be there to ensure that you travel safely and that you are able to reenter your body without any difficulty. Also, if you meditate to expand your consciousness, you may speak this sentence before beginning your meditation, with one minor alteration: "Archangel Uriel, come to me in my altered state and expand my consciousness in preparation for transmutation."

I would like to take a moment now and explain what transmutation may feel like. It happens at the snap of your fingers. It does not hurt; death itself is not painful. The process of the human body may be painful (i.e., cancer and various unnatural ways the death of the physical body happens are painful). But at the moment of transmutation, you do not feel pain. It is almost like slipping into a dream state—but it is not a dream. It is the next stage of the cycle, in which you carry all the lessons and knowledge you have learned (or have not learned) and gained from this lifetime to your higher self. By working with me, you will recognize me and my energy. I will be there for you as you pass and ensure that you recognize the journey you are about to take.

I understand that some people reading this are wondering what "God" is like. I placed that name in quotations because humans think that God is a man, that he has very specific features, and that he will take very specific actions. While I appreciate the time that humans put into their devotion of God, I would like to call this energy Spirit. Like me and other energies, Spirit is neither male nor female. In fact, Spirit is a feeling. Spirit is all encompassing. It is spoken to, and speaks through, feelings. There is no need to communicate with Spirit using words. Spirit understands all with a mere thought. You understand this upon transmutation. You also understand that Spirit has no end and no beginning. Spirit is an absolute circle. I know humans believe that time is linear and that this concept may be difficult to configure. And if that is so, do not worry. Even if you never understand this while in human form, you will understand this upon transmutation.

Some humans will read this and believe that this book, my explanations, and my statements are perhaps blasphemous. That is perfectly fine. That is a very human response when you are a person who does not like yourself or your beliefs challenged. You may close this book and move on with your life. To that person, I say that you will find out when you pass that what I am explaining is true and accurate. I do not judge you. I appreciate you and your human response. For that is what humans do; they have opinions. Because I have never been a human, I truly love communicating with you and watching your development.

What should you expect upon transmutation? First and foremost, after my energy transfer and practicing increasing your frequency and expanding your consciousness, you will have an idea of what it will feel like. At the moment of transmutation, you will feel peace and comfort. By recognizing my energy, there will be no need for you to feel confused or like you have unfinished business in your human form. By increasing your vibrational frequency and expanding your consciousness, you will begin living differently. You will begin having conversations that perhaps would have been considered uncomfortable. But you will know that you should have them. You will be able to connect with other humans and energies in a way that lets you speak freely and know that you will not leave any conversations until the last minute. You will be able to pass from your human body happily and with the knowledge that you have lived in a way that was all encompassing.

There are many reasons why some people are unable to pass on. They remain in human forms and on the plane and dimension in which their human forms died. One main reason is that they feel that there is unfinished business here. This unfinished business may be in the form of a conversation (i.e., they never told people how they really felt). By increasing your vibrational frequency and expanding your consciousness, you will know that certain conversations must be had while you are in human form. Upon passing, you will not feel like you need to tell someone for the last time how much you loved him or her. Your life will become much easier, in that you will no longer fear death or the process of transmutation. By practicing expanding your consciousness in either the dream state or meditation, you will be experiencing what that process will feel like. And you will not have any stress or anxiety about the unknown.

Because I am close to my page limitation—the transcriptionist has given each of us energies ten pages to communicate our sentiments on—I want to make mention of something. When you are practicing expanding your consciousness and after you make the statement regarding your intention to me, think about the other energies that you would like to help guide and meet you upon initially transmuting. Do you have any pets that have passed on? Perhaps you have a favorite aunt, uncle, or parent. Start voicing whom you would like to see in that initial step. By letting those energies know that you would like to see them upon your initial steps out of your human body, you will be able to call them to you. Although it is very easy for spirits to come to you quickly, it is still so much more respectful to let them know that you would like to see them. You make appointments as a human. Why shouldn't you make appointments as you exit your human body? It is still a respectful thing to do in spirit form.

I will shortly be giving the reins back to Anubis. If you would like more information from me, just let me know. (I hear all human requests). Just reach out to me with your third eye. Perhaps listen to the frequency of 528 hertz. I will take all requests into consideration. I will then reach out to this transcriptionist or another. I am happy to have been able to participate in this book and for you to have read my commentary about transmutation. Thank you.

COMMENTARY BY ANUBIS

At the end of each chapter, I will provide some commentary and transition to the next one. Archangel Uriel gave their explanation and thoughts about how you as a human may prepare for transmutation. I am aware that many people recognize the word *archangel* and have an immediate thought about what that means. Perhaps after reading their words, your thoughts have changed. That is good. We, as energies, are not to be pigeonholed into a specific vision. We do have characteristics that have been written down by humans from time to time. Perhaps these humans have had visions in which we have appeared to them. You might be thinking, *I thought that I had a vision or saw Archangel Uriel at one point, but it couldn't have been. Because Archangel Uriel didn't look anything like the way he was drawn by an illustration.* Here's the thing: The way one human interprets a vision of us is not the only interpretation of the way we present ourselves.

For example, when this transcriptionist has visions, certain energies appear to her in two-dimensional form. Let's say she had a vision of me. She draws the version of me that she saw. Do you think that I appear to everyone as a cartoonish form? Certainly not. That is just how her brain interprets these visits or visions. Another human brain will interpret the way I appear much differently.

This next energy, Xia, will have a very different commentary from Archangel Uriel. Xia (pronounced zee-a) is what you would call an alien. She is a very revered high priestess from Zeta Reticuli. I know that some of you will read the word *alien* and immediately become nervous or afraid. Others will read "Zeta Reticuli" and automatically feel nervous or afraid. I ask that you reserve judgment until you read her chapter. Or you can skip over it if you like. But if you have picked up this book, you are likely open-minded or at the very least, a bit curious as to what an alien has to say about transmutation. While some of you have had experience with Pleiadians or Andromedans, the stories of any human experiences with the Zeta Reticuli have often been negative in nature. Xia is from the Zeta Reticuli race, which has not yet been explored—the white zetas. Unfortunately, the grays have given many zetas a negative connotation. But I assure you that there is no energy involved with this guide, who would be considered negative.

Because Xia is a high priestess, her explanation and chapter will be based on a few rituals. I will let her explain in more detail, but she has a connection to the Witch. Xia and the Witch also have a very strong connection to the transcriptionist. Again, please reserve any judgment for later. However, I assure you that learning about the white zetas will be very interesting. I do not believe that any humans have been contacted by one yet (or at least not one who has written about it).

If you have read Archangel Uriel's chapter, I recommend that you give yourself a few minutes before reading Xia's. As part of your earlier signed contract, I also recommend that you ask for me to conduct another energy transfer for the purpose of increasing your vibrational frequency and getting you attuned to reading Xia's words. Just say the following three times: *"Anubis, I am requesting energetic preparation for meeting Xia."* Then lie down for a few minutes in silence, breathing in and out steadily. Perhaps after this energy transfer, you will need to place this book to the side for a moment. If that is how you are feeling, please do so. This attunement may feel differently from Archangel Uriel's energy.

Also, here is a bit of a warning. Some humans may take this information and/or energy transfer(s) and use them for malicious purposes. Please know that by doing so, there will be consequences. With that, we journey on with Xia.

CHAPTER 2

XIA

I'd like to say hello again (to some of you). And it's nice to meet others. I am so pleased not only to meet all of you but also to be the one to introduce you to my race: the white Zetas. Some of you may have heard of another faction of Zetas, which you refer to as the Grays. The Grays are known because they have had contact with humans for centuries. Unfortunately, their contact has been looked upon as being negative. It's unfortunate, not because of how humans have thought of the Grays but because of how the Grays have interacted with you. I am what you could call a future form of the Zeta race. As Archangel Uriel explained, time is a circle. And with certain technology, one may get in touch with the universal energy (UE) and know the past, present, and future. I am able to communicate with you through UE. Through UE, I am going to guide you into being able to begin and to understand transmutation. I have experienced transmutation an infinite number of times, not only because I have lived an infinite number of lives but also because I am able to tap into UE and re-experience it from those past lives. I am also able to jump forward in time and experience it in future lifetimes. If you choose to, you will be able to do so after reading this chapter.

Let me begin by saying that the transcriptionist, The Witch, Kali, and I are very interconnected. So if you have chosen the number two, you have likely known one or more of us in the lifetime you are currently in or in a past or future lifetime. You would not have known one of us as just an acquaintance but as something more—perhaps a relative, lover, or lifelong friend. I will let The Witch speak for herself, but I will just say that in that capacity, you would have likely been in her coven. While I am a high priestess, that term (high priestess) has a slightly different meaning for The Witch than it does for me. As a high priestess in the galactic federation of light, I preside as a force of energy to give guidance (through energy) to the federation. I do engage in rituals. Through those rituals, I explain the energy that the federation must focus on at different times. I am a seer. (Perhaps for you, this would mean a clairvoyant.) I am also telepathic. Some humans have a perception that all aliens are telepathic. This is incorrect. It is a specific gift, which is granted to us. We must work with and refine it. I have various other gifts, which we will discuss throughout this chapter.

Because some of you are not familiar with the federation, I will take a minute to explain it. The federation is a council, which is made up of civilizations from many different planets, galaxies, and universes. We work together for the harmonious existence of all life. There is a federation in each of the inhabited galaxies of our universe. These federations are part of the universal-management structure, much like field offices are part of the management structure for a large corporation. The federation for the Milky Way galaxy is called the Galactic Federation of Light, but some of the races represented in this federation may call it by other names; hence the difference in the names given by the Zetas, Andromedans, etc. Each race, civilization, and planet has a council within the federation to represent it. These councils vary in size depending on population as well as the amount of responsibilities they carry within the management structure of the federation. There are literally thousands of these councils because there are many races represented. I know that this topic may be of interest to some of you. But because this guide is not about alien races and their incorporation into the federation, this topic will not be covered much here. I know that there are other resources, though, for those of you who would like to learn more about this topic.

I am also part of a larger federation, one of which incorporates energy from every galaxy. I am the energy from the Milky Way's federation. I am able to be part of this larger federation due to my telepathic abilities. I am also able to use the astral plane and project a certain amount of particles from myself to another place in time. You will not be learning how to do this, but some of you are able to do so. You just don't know yet that you have this ability.

Let me give you some information about the white Zetas. As I stated, we are a future race of the Zetas. I feel so much sadness for those who have had negative encounters with the Grays. Please understand that all races mature. At that stage of our race, we had very little emotion. Although our intentions were not to harm you but to assist the human race's development, we know that it was not done properly. I liken it to human experimentation on animals. As you have progressed, you (or those of you who have increased your frequency) understand that such experimentation is wrong and cruel. We also have that same understanding regarding the Grays. Later in this chapter, there is an option for you to receive an energy transfer from me. And should you choose to accept that transfer, you may invoke me if you ever encounter a Gray. In that moment, I will be able to guide the Gray into understanding that what they are doing may be done only with consent from a human. There are humans who do not mind this experimentation; they willingly comply and have made that clear to the Grays.

Also, I am not the color white. I am blue with a white aura. White is a monochromatic color, which goes well with primary, secondary, and tertiary colors. It provides a soothing effect, making other colors stand out, particularly brighter ones. It is associated with light, goodness, safety, brilliance, illumination, and understanding. The Zetas have evolved from the color gray to the color blue. Your race will have some color shifts also. It is just part of evolution. So if you would like to have an image of me in your head as you read through this chapter, please do not envision me as the color white. I am blue. Now, before an energy transfer from me to you takes place, let's tune into the vibrational frequency that is created when my energy combines with the number two.

As stated in the introduction to this guide, the number two is known as a supremely feminine force. It is one that represents both grace and power. It is cooperative, and it always aims at bringing peace and balance back to a relationship or situation. The number two also represents sensitivity. Of all the numbers, it has the strongest intuition. It is able to sense currents and feelings instinctively. Then it uses those clues to connect with others empathically. So if you have chosen this number, you may be instinctively guided to the divine feminine energy. You are also likely to be empathic. Now, I know that there are some of you saying, *"There's no way I'm empathic. I do not have the ability to connect with others."* I answer you in this way: You are likely extremely empathic. Most empaths block the emotions of others instinctively. This is a defense mechanism. If you were not able to block out the emotions of other energies, you would likely hide in a corner and never come out. You understand that there are so many energies out there that in order to survive, you must block them out. With my help, you will be able to know how to open those gates when you choose to do so. It is entirely within your power to let in a single energy or multiple energies. Feeling the emotions of others can be draining. And you are instinctively blocking those for purposes of your own survival and well-being.

My energy combined with that of the number two measures in at one thousand hertz. At this frequency, you are able to restore all seven chakras at once. Please feel free to tune into this frequency while you are reading this chapter. I will also be giving an energy transfer that will allow you to feel this balance throughout your body. You will also be able to call on me to restore all seven chakras at once afterward. I will give you these tools throughout this chapter. The following image represents the one-thousand-hertz frequency.

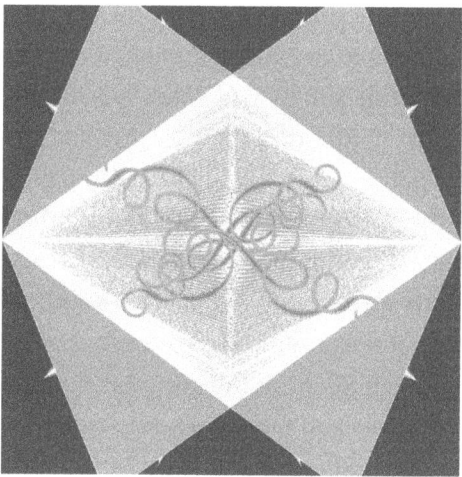

Frequency

If you would like to receive this energy transfer, please look at this mandala for as long as you wish. You do not have to, but it might be beneficial to tune into this frequency using your internet during the energy transfer. While looking at this mandala (and perhaps while listening to the one-thousand-hertz frequency), state the following two times: *"I wish for and accept the energy coming from Xia, the high priestess and white Zeta. As I decree, so mote it be."* You will be able to feel your chakras opening. For many of you, this energy transfer will not cause your kundalini to unravel. That takes time. Some of you who are reading this will get to that level. Some of you have kundalinis that are able to do (or close to doing so). In Hinduism, the kundalini (translation: coiled snake) is a form of divine feminine energy, which is located at the base of the spine. When this energy in the body is cultivated and awakened, it may lead to spiritual liberation. The transcriptionist once had a dream in which she was holding a samurai sword. At the base of this sword was a coiled snake. At times in her dream, the snake would uncoil around the sword, and the head of the snake would make its way toward the end of the sword. Then the snake would recoil around the handle of the sword. This represented her kundalini uncoiling around her spine. Be sure to look for such imagery in your dreams or meditations. As it did for the transcriptionist, such things are likely to be a representation of your kundalini uncoiling. The kundalini will be mentioned by many of the guides in this book. But Kwan Yen will be discussing it the most in Chapter Six.

Tuning into this frequency will also assist you with the additional energy transfer from me. This next energy transfer differs from the one above. The transfer described above involves the opening of all seven chakras. It is the energy of one thousand hertz. This next transfer is coming from me to directly assist you with the process that this guide states: transmutation. As indicated earlier, I will be taking you through the past and to the future. By doing this, you will be able to experience transmutation as you have felt it before and how you will feel it after.

I understand and know why many of you may be hesitant for this transfer. The Grays have given my race a very negative connotation and rightly so. But as Anubis stated earlier in this guide, I am from the light. I would not be able to get past Anubis and to the transcriptionist for her to channel me if I were not from the light. Although my energy transfer is not necessary for you to continue, it will make the next part of my chapter (going into the past and the future) much easier. So if you would like an energy transfer from me, please focus on this symbol:

Mandala

While focusing on this symbol, state the following three times: *"Through the past and into the future I wish to go. Xia, your energy transfer please bestow. Provide a compass within my mind so that in the darkness a light will shine. Not just north, south, east, and west, but a compass for dimensions we shall manifest. As I decree, so mote it be."* You might feel a tingling sensation at the base of your neck. If you do not, don't worry. You are still receiving this energy transfer. Now, we are going to use the following symbol for the purpose of traveling the astral plane.

X

The astral plane is the world of the celestial spheres. It is crossed by the soul in its astral body on the way to its being born and after death. It is generally believed to be populated by angels, spirits, or other immaterial beings. Astral projection (also known as astral travel) is a term used to describe an intentional out-of-body experience, which assumes the existence of a subtle body called an astral body, through which consciousness can function separately from the physical body and travel throughout the astral plane. Some readers may have adverse reactions to these terms. It might help to think of the astral plan as the quantum field. According to the laws of physics, the fundamental building blocks of nature are not discrete particles. Instead, they are continuous fluidlike substances that are spread throughout space. We call these objects fields. The most familiar examples of fields are the electric and magnetic fields. The ripples in these fields give rise to what we call light or more generally, electromagnetic waves. The quantum field contains all of physics. The field can describe vast numbers of particles, which interact in a myriad of ways. Put in the simplest of terms, the quantum field is everything and nothing at the same time.

We will be using the above symbol to pick the time that your astral body (or consciousness) will be traveling to. As your guide, please picture me as a blue ball of light with a white aura. When you see a blue ball of light with a white aura, you will know that I am there with you, guiding you. If you do not see me, do not worry. I might be behind or above you, guiding you through your crown chakra. Now, picture the above symbol in three-dimensional form. Please note that the above symbol is a sort of compass. We are not using the normal type of compass (north, south, east, or west) but rather, a cross-sectional compass (northeast, southeast, southwest, and northwest). As evolution takes place, this compass will be used in the future. As the Earth evolves, these cross sections will become the new main directions. Perhaps you will be some of the first to become used to these as the new directions.

Using your crown chakra, open yourself up to the quantum field. As you look through the quantum field, pick a place within it. Let your consciousness drift and guide you to an area within the quantum field. If you are having trouble picking a specific point, you may ask me to guide your consciousness to an area within the quantum field. Take as long as you like. Remember the one-thousand-hertz vibrational frequency. Listen to it as your consciousness picks a particular location within the quantum field. Once you have picked your location, take the three-dimensional compass and wrap it around the area. Make sure that it is able to rotate. Look at the compass with your crown chakra and pick a location on the southwest axis. We are picking the southwest axis because south represents the spark of life, intense or gentle heat, and illumination. West represents completion and a definitive understanding of our own mortality. It symbolizes the movement from ignorance to wisdom. Sometimes called the little death, West asks us to put away our childish ways and to evolve to become our most sage self. And so, it is on this axis that we will find a past life.

Once you have picked exactly where you would like to focus on this axis, give yourself some time to become comfortable with this travel. Allowing your consciousness to travel in this way can make you lightheaded. So if you feel a bit lightheaded, take some time to focus and allow yourself to become acquainted with this frequency. Once you are comfortable at this frequency, and once you have picked your spot on the southwest access of the compass, picture that axis lined with golden doorways. There are an infinite number of doors. Now examine the door that you are looking at. Is there a number, symbol, or picture at the top? The label on the door will give you access to this particular door in the future (i.e., you will remember it by finding the label that you see right now). After examining the marking, go ahead and open the door. As you open the door, take note of what you are looking at. Is it in black and white or in color? Perhaps you see a book floating in the air. Some people may see a video clip running. Perhaps you see a television. Or perhaps you step into the actual world behind that door.

The next step is to take hold of the time and ensure that it is happening at a pace you are able to interpret. Time moves very differently on different planes and/or dimensions. If you see a book, make sure that the pages are not flipping at a pace that is slow enough for you to be able to decipher what is written on each page. If you see a video clip, make sure it is not running at a speed where you are unable to view what is being shown. If you have entered the body that you possessed behind this door, make sure that your actions are not happening at light speed. That may happen when you view past lives in this manner.

Now it is time to view the past life. Start at the beginning with the tool you have made for yourself. Are you on Earth?[1] If so, what was the name you were given? Are you in a desert land or a cold tundra? Are you viewing this from a bird's eye view or inhabiting the body that was once yours? (Because time is a circle, you are still inhabiting this body, so it is not difficult for you to come back to it right now.) Experience that life as you once did. Accept the struggles and hardships that you may have had. Those things play a significant role in your following lives. You are meant to go through struggles and hardships. You will have to keep reincarnating until you have lived through things like illness (both

---

[1] You could be viewing a life in which you are not human. You could have been in a number of different alien races and planets. Many of you have likely lived at least one life in another form. I will list some of them here. I am placing this information in a footnote because I recognize that some humans either already know this information or perhaps are not ready yet to know it.

1. Lyrians are thought to be the mother race of all intelligent races. Lyrians are thought to be responsible for the seeding of many other cultures and races.
2. Arcturians are a highly evolved race and are well-known for their power of healing. Arcturians are also able to accomplish additional powers through the aid of their mastery of the conscious mind.
3. Pleiadians are a benevolent race and are closely related to but more emotionally and spiritually developed than humans. They are interested in helping humanity on its own evolutionary journey.
4. Andromedans are forty-five-thousand years ahead of humans and are technologically and spiritually advanced. It is thought that Andromedans are the descendants of Lyrians. They are a very loving, wise, and beautiful star race. Andromedan star seeds are thought to play an important role on Earth.
5. Vegans are able to communicate with humans by a form of telepathy. Their language has been described as sounding like a bird's song. Only the intended listeners will understand the meaning of what the Vegan is saying. Vegans are thought to be the personification of compassion.

There are many other alien races. I have named just a few here. There are many books and resources that you may look at if you see yourself in a different format while in a past or future life. This guide is not only about other alien races.

physical and mental), financial difficulties, etc. You must live through these things so that the universe (through you) understands how to combat darkness during times of hardship. Perhaps you succumbed to darkness in certain lives. This is also significant, both for you and the universe. If you succumbed to darkness, you may need to go through that life again until you are able to work through those experiences, and you come out of it being reunited with the light (or the Source). Parts of you may be fractured. You will need to guide your past self (or have someone else guide your past self) back to your higher self.

Experience everything you once did. As you near the end of this life, slow everything down. Turn the pages slower. Make the film proceed in slow motion. Become conscious of yourself if you are experiencing everything firsthand versus secondhand (i.e., reading a book or watching a film). See yourself as you once were. Are you older? Or perhaps you have only reached twelve years of age. At this point, if you are reading this book, you have likely experienced death at a very young age. Watch that moment in which your body begins failing. Or perhaps it is the moment that you are engaged in a battle or childbirth. Whatever it may be, you are able to tell that this is the moment when your consciousness transmutes because you are nearing the end of the book or film. Or you are conscious that your experience within this past self is at the end of its time. Whatever it may be, you are going to experience the moment when your past self decided to transmute. It happens in the blink of an eye. There is absolutely no pain associated with transmutation. Your consciousness knows this. Now your current consciousness is able to intelligently compute this past experience.

When you are ready to leave what you have mapped out in the quantum field, take note of where your compass is so that you may come back to the other points on the axis whenever you would like to. You may also take your compass with you (the three-dimensional version). To do this, wrap your consciousness around it. You may ask for my help to implant it within your pineal gland. The pineal gland is a small, pea-shaped gland in your brain. Its function isn't fully understood, but researchers know that it produces and regulates some hormones, including melatonin. By secreting the hormone melatonin, the pineal gland helps regulate your body's circadian rhythm. In ancient Egypt, the pineal gland was known as the seat of the spirit or the soul. Ancient Egyptians used the third eye as a route to higher awareness and consciousness. Some religions equate the pineal gland to spiritual awakening. Other religions connect it to the third eye, which represents intuition and clairvoyance. By implanting your compass into your pineal gland, you will download the information contained within it. When you wish to revisit it and consciously retain the knowledge within it, you only need to locate it within your pineal gland. Although this information was already accessible to you, now you have a conscious memory of where it has been placed so that you may access it as quickly as you would like.

If you would like for me to implant your compass in your pineal gland, make your intention clear. To do this, please state, "*Xia, help guide me. Take my compass from the quantum field and make a pathway from the quantum field to my pineal gland. As I decree, so mote it be.*" As I do this, focus on your pineal gland (in the middle of your brain). Breathe in slowly three times, hold it for three, and breathe out for three. Continue to focus on your pineal gland and be conscious of your breathing for three minutes. Once three minutes have passed, become conscious of your body. Breathe in and out slowly and come back to where you are. Perhaps you are lying in bed, and you have a window nearby. Listen to the sounds that are around you. Perhaps it is silent or you have music playing in the background. As you come back to your body, wiggle your hands and toes. Move your face muscles. Open and close your mouth to stretch your jaw muscles. Slowly open your eyes. You have now successfully stored your compass within your pineal gland.

Let's go over what you may find on the other axis. If you travel to the southeast axis, you will be accessing your future lives. As you already know, south represents the spark of life, intense or gentle heat, and illumination. It also represents transformation. East represents a new day and a new beginning. It represents dawn, hopefulness, and inceptions. The energies of the East inspire our personal divinity, wisdom, and spiritual potential. As you may guess, your journeys to your future lives on the southeast axis are infinite. Because time is a circle (as represented by your compass), you may access your future lives and experience the transmutation of your consciousness in a different manner. I say that it's in a different manner because like everything, your consciousness evolves. Because you have experienced a past instance of transmutation while in your current form, your consciousness has just evolved. Experiencing transmutation of consciousness in the future will evolve your current consciousness even more. If or when you decide to experience the transmutation of your future consciousness, you may invoke my assistance. You may do this by stating the following three times: "*Xia, my consciousness invokes your guidance to assist with my accessing the southeast axis on my compass. As I decree, so mote it be.*"

The northern parts of the compass are very different. The northwest and northeast axes contain the possibilities of each life. The northwest axis contains the infinite possibilities of past lives, and the northeast axis contains the possibilities of future lives. I recommend waiting to travel to those axes until you are comfortable with visiting the south axes. Inviting information such as that contained within the northern axes could lead to confusion and misunderstanding. Invoking me to assist you with your journey will help. I will be able to block any information that could lead you to feeling confused. Just repeat the sentence above and replace "southeast" with the axis you wish my assistance to visit.

I do believe I am coming to the end of my ten pages. I hope you have enjoyed this experience as much as I have. Again, I cannot stress enough the importance of the message of forgiveness in the process of evolution. The human race will evolve, but the race of the zetas has already done so. One day, perhaps humankind will (as a whole) seek forgiveness from the many animals that it has used for experimentation. The thought that your intelligence places you above another race or species is what led to the Grays believing that experimenting on humans was okay.

Reading this chapter (along with this book) will assist you with the evolution of your consciousness. I hope that this is the start of your journey or just one of the many points that your journey has reached. Thank you.

COMMENTARY BY ANUBIS

Well now, that was certainly a journey, wasn't it? Xia exemplifies what humans should aspire to be: foregoing her ego in favor of love, peace, and compassion. Some people will still see Reticulies as scary or negative. Those emotions have their basis in fear. And fear is exactly what holds you back from evolution. Preconceived notions of heaven and hell, good and evil, and what is righteous and what is not. These concepts are human creations. While there is an underworld (I rule it, so I should know), there is no world where everything rains fire and brimstone, and an amorphous creature named "The Devil" creates chaos for all humans. Thank you, Xia, for allowing your energy to be felt.

The next chapter is The Morrigan/Crow Magick. As you will see, this chapter will either strike a note with you or it will not. You will either feel a connection immediately or you will not. The Morrigan is steeped in folklore. Some of that folklore is true, and some is sort of true. I believe it is The Morrigan's wish to delve into animal totems and how becoming connected with animal spirits helps one's consciousness transmute. Humans connected to animals might find this chapter comforting.

As with Xia, The Morrigan will ask that you place your superstitions behind you. While she is connected to witchcraft and magick, The Witch will be using Chapter Eight to use those means for the purpose of transmutation. Although The Morrigan may use some spells and magick, it will be tangential; it's only for you to use to connect with animal spirits. And so, with that, please be prepared to meet The Morrigan.

CHAPTER 3

THE MORRIGAN/CROW MAGIC

Dia dhuit.[2] I am so pleased and happy to be speaking with you through these pages. At this moment, while these pages are being transcribed, "Canon in D" is playing in the background. Can you hear it? When you work with me, I consider it to be a marriage of energies and an exchange of promises. A divorce will never be a part of this picture. But in exchange, you will receive unending favor from me. You will also receive strength and love. I have many marriages. There are three versions of me. Some think of this as three sisters. If that is how you wish to think of me that is fine. But it is really more of a marriage for eternity. I am the maiden, the mother, and the crone. Men who seek to invoke me must have been with me in a past life (and he is likely to have been female). And in this lifetime, that male must have very feminine energy. There seems to be an imbalance in this world of yours. Men seem to think that they can take what they want from women when they want it. Men glorify violence against women. There are movies that have developed from fantasies of men who wish to ingrain these types of actions into your culture. These "men" are not really men. They will be pets at some point—perhaps my pets. As Anubis stated, you will either

---

[2] Dia dhuit is an Irish greeting. Audrey Nickel, *Irish Gaeliic Greetings*, https://www.bitesize.irish/blog/irish-gaelic-greetings/.

connect with me or you will not. And it would seem that any male who began to read this book has likely moved on (unless there is a strong female energy about him). Although this book is about transmutation, I also seek to plant some seeds to grow a different culture for you humans. Men have tied women's hands, and they want them to be quiet. They will not be quiet. Violence against women is a way to keep women's true potentials down. Men know this. They know that women have a greater ability to use their intuitions. And that, combined with intelligence, scares men. So they seek to subdue us. But women are also better at transmuting their consciousness (because of their ability to have greater intuition). And so we have much more "success" on this other side of the veil. If you are in need of healing because of violence or actions done to you because of a man, you may use the ceremony described within the next few pages to invoke me and then to heal. Know that you will get there. As I said, men who do this kind of thing in this world will answer for their actions in the next.

Before we begin, I am going to address the number three. Three is the number of creativity, communication, and expression. Numerologists recognize that three is the number of the child. It symbolizes the growth and magic that results from the combination of two other things. It's the metaphorical child brought forth from two parents, who is full of energy and possibility. This number is the fruit of your labors. It carries spiritual meaning, power, and an abundance of energy. The number three is quite important when working with magick. We say certain phrases three times. Any witch knows that any working should be completed before three full or new moons (depending on the request). I am a triple goddess in that I have three forms (as noted above). So when working with me, the number three is important because it encompasses each one of my forms.

My frequency, when combined with the number three comes to 333 hertz, which is the pleasure frequency for women. It is said that it is the only car frequency that raises their testosterone. The 333-hertz frequency is said to recalibrate your DNA, opening up some sort of new consciousness for the listener. This frequency could quite possibly be one of the most angelic, as it is a master number. Please feel free to find a link on the internet that allows you to listen to the 333-hertz frequency while reading this chapter or connecting with me. It is quite calming. Again, if you are a male without an abundance of feminine energy, you may not actually get to connect with me.[3]

Now, let's transfer some energy. As stated earlier, I have a connection to The Witch. My energy (and therefore one of my lifetimes, was led as Morgana (King Arthur's supernatural sister)). I will leave some of the rituals for The Witch. But I will need you to complete a ritual for my energy transfer. To begin, you will need the following:

- A purple candle
- Olive oil
- Rosemary
- A plate or a little container
- Incense (any kind will do)
- Some sort of depiction of a crow (you could even draw one on a piece of paper yourself)

Place these items on a table in accordance with the picture below. (You will need them all.) In ceremonial style, light the candle. Walk around the table clockwise three times while stating the following: "With this candle, I invoke The Morrigan."

Now, light the incense. Walk around the table clockwise while stating, "With this incense, I invoke The Morrigan." Place the depiction of a crow on the table. (You will be making a triangle with the candle, incense, and crow.)

---

[3] A normal, healthy body should resonate with a natural frequency of sixty-five to seventy-five megahertz. While it might be surreal to think about, it means that humans generate electromagnetic energy or noise even as we're just standing in place. When exposed to higher frequencies, such as those found in frequency healing, the human body is stimulated to heal itself.

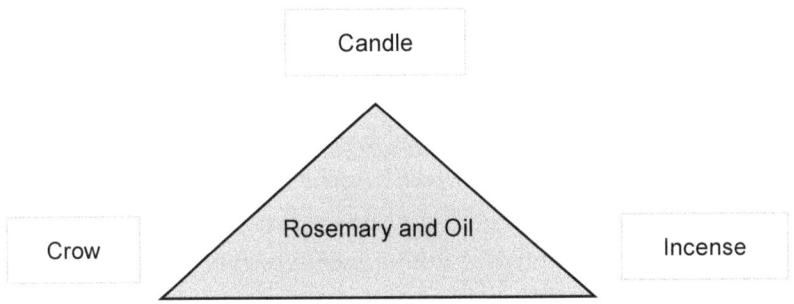

As you walk around the table (again clockwise and again three times), state the following: "With this crow, I invoke The Morrigan."

Now, place the container in the center of the triangle (as depicted above). Pour the oil and drop the rosemary inside. Place your hands over it and state the following three times: "With this ceremony, I invoke The Morrigan." Leave your hands over the container for as long as you wish. You may close your eyes if you wish. If you do, what do you see behind them? If you see me, what form am I taking—the maid, mother, or crone? Perhaps you see all three of me. Feel that energy and focus it through your hands and into the oil and rosemary. When you feel like you are done, place your hands over your eyes. Now what do you see? A triangle? A crow? Just breathe in and out and feel the energy as it moves through you. When you are done, blow on your hands three times.

You may do what you wish with the picture, candle, and incense. You may use this ritual again as many times as you wish. We will be using the container with the oil and the rosemary again, so keep that in a safe place. (You will be using it for meditative journeys or before you go to sleep.)

Before getting to the next part of using the oil and rosemary (called Morrigan's Magick), I want to explain what we will be doing with it. As stated earlier, you will become one or get in touch with the animal world. You will come into contact with your totem. Animal totems are connections to a specific animal. They have been chosen to guide you through life (like a spirit guide, only spirit guides were once human).

Your animal totem represents qualities, abilities, and characteristics that you currently have or that you are in the process of developing.

This animal may be connected to you through a past life. If you were a witch, perhaps it was your familiar. I understand that in the modern world, people think that they need a bear, lion, or cheetah as an animal totem. That is pure poppycock! Your totem may be anything from the animal world—even animals that have gone extinct on the Earth. When picking an animal totem, you might be drawn to a unicorn, dragon, or phoenix. But don't forget about energies like grasshoppers or stink bugs. As I just stated, you do not need a bear to be fierce. Slugs make magnificent totems. Rats and possums do too. Do not conform yourself to earthbound animals or those that you believe one must need to have an experience.

You may have already guessed that one of my totems is the majestic crow. You and your animal totem share certain characteristics. If the crow is your animal totem, these are some traits that you share.

- Inner knowledge
- Introspection
- Heightened Intuition
- Creativity
- Self-Awareness
- Magick
- Shapeshifting
- Transformation

Perhaps you are someone who sees a lot of rabbits, maybe even on a daily basis. Or perhaps you often have dreams of rabbits leading you to places or getting you to safety. Some character traits of having a rabbit as your totem are

- Fearful or anxious
- Abundant
- Clever and swift

- Creative
- Fertile
- Spontaneous

This guide or book is blessed by the pig totem. Pigs are considered the smartest barnyard animal. They can be trained with ease and often faster than dogs can be. Because few people get to spend any time with these amazing creatures, they underestimate the pig's intelligence. Also, pigs do not care what others think. This creature doesn't worry about who sees how smart they are or whether anyone acknowledges pig's intelligence. Pig just keeps plowing forward and living life. Pig represents

- Abundance
- Good luck
- Fertility
- Forward movement
- Forward thinking
- Sincerity
- Determination

Your animal totem is going to be very important, so picking yours must be done with care and patience. The first step is to think about whether there seems to be a particular type of animal energy that is attracted to you. When I say "attracted to," I mean the following: Do you seem to see a particular animal more than others? Is it a particular bird? Do cats seem to make their way to you? Or have you always been interested in a particular animal? I know there is something called *Shark Week* on a certain channel at times. Are you drawn to watching sharks? What about whales?

While having a general animal totem is fine (i.e., spider, shark, whale, etc.), you can also have a very specific animal totem. There are an incredible number of different spiders. You could have a black-widow spider as your totem. The same is true with sharks and whales. Although a general shark is fine to have as your totem, you could also have the great-white, hammerhead, or tiger shark. To start, however, it might be easier to begin with a general totem.

The first use of Morrigan's Magick will be using it to connect with the crow or the raven. As I indicated earlier, I am a shapeshifter, and I enjoy taking the form of a crow. I also enjoy taking the shape of a raven. Ravens and crows are different.

Characteristics	Ravens	Crows
Size	Larger (24–27 inches)	Smaller (17–21 inches)
Weight	Heavier (1.5–4.5 pounds)	Lighter (0.6–1.1 pounds)
Color	Shiny black plumage	Matte-black plumage
Tail Shape	Wedge-shaped tail	Fan-shaped tail
Wing Shape	More pointed angular wings	More uniform rounded wings
Calls	Deeper, croaking, "Cronk"	Higher-pitched, cawing: "Caw"
Vocalization	Known for a variety of calls	Fewer vocalizations, simpler
Behavior	Solitary or in small groups	Often seen in larger groups
Range	Found in more remote areas	Common in urban and suburban areas
Habitat	Mountainous and forested	Varied, adaptable to environments
Intelligence	Considered more intelligent	Considered highly intelligent
Diet	Opportunistic, diverse diet	Scavengers, varied diet
Life Span	Longer life span (20–30 years)	Shorter life span (7–8 years)

Character traits of a raven are

- Introspection
- Inner knowledge
- Self-awareness

- Creativity
- Shapeshifting
- Magick
- Sexuality
- Divination

While many similar traits are shared with crow, there are some minor differences. This matters because in this next section, you are going to merge with me. I will be in the shape of either a crow or a raven. You might want to look at some pictures of each of the birds so that you will be able to identify the one you will be merging with. The ritual above where I transferred some energy to you will assist with your ability to merge with the crow or raven. You may have seen a crow or a raven during the energy transfer. This next exercise will be different, however, because you will be merging with me while I am in the form of a crow or raven. By doing this, you will begin to learn how to transmute your consciousness.

To merge with me when I am in the form of a crow or raven, you will need a few tools. (Yes, there is another ritual.) In this ritual, you will need Morrigan's Magick. You are going to need four items. Each item represents one of the directions. Below is a chart indicating what each direction represents and items that you might wish to choose. However, you will sit and have Morrigan's Magick in the center. This chart will also assist you with the Witch's chapter.

Direction	Element	Associations	Colors	Items
North	Earth	Winter, foundation, ancestors, protection, security, job, money, family, friends, and culture	Dark green, ivy, browns, and golds	Broom, flowers, coins, bark, dirt, rocks, tourmaline, onyx, emeralds, and moss agate

East	Air	Spring, clarity, intelligence, freedom, thought, word, deed, truth, justice, rationality, and taking action	Pastels— light green or blue— white, and light-to- medium yellow	Wand, feathers, bubbles, a pinwheel, a journal, and incense
South	Fire	Summer, passion, motivation, creativity, lust, enlightenment, transformation, and willpower	Red, orange, and dark yellow	Athame, incense, candle, chili peppers, and firecrackers
West	Water	Autumn, emotions, love, following your heart, the moon and the tides, all the psychic abilities, timing, rhythm, the subconscious, and the process of healing	Blue (medium and dark) and turquois	Chalice, wineglass, water, wine, and seashells
Center	Divinity	Where all the above comes together and interconnectedness	Purple (may be skipped for merging with the crow or raven)	Morrigan's Magick

When you have gathered the items representing each of your quarters (north, east, south, and west), place each of them at the correct location and recite the following. (You should be in the center and facing each direction as you place your item down.)

> To the Witch of the East,
> May your clarity run deep.
> May you guard the air and all the secrets it keeps.

May you find inspiration through thought, word, and deed.
As this has always been, so mote it be.

   Place the item down.

To the Witch of the South,
May your courage run deep.
May you guard the fire and all the secrets it keeps.
May you lead with passion and fire's ardent energy.
As it has always been, so mote it be.

   Place the item down.

To the Witch of the West,
May your happiness run deep.
May you guard the waters and the secrets it keeps.
May you balance and keep pure emotions and femininity.
As it has always been, so mote it be.

   Place the item down.

To the Witch of the North,
May your empathy run deep.
And may you guard the Earth and all the secrets it keeps.
May you find strength in Earth's soil and trees.
As this has always been, so mote it be.

   Place the item down.

To the Goddess of all, our Center, our Light,
You are the Sun and the Moon,
Guarding all,
Day and Night.
Thank you for crow magick and for accepting me.
As it has always been, so mote it be.

Place the item down in the center and sit in the center. Open the container that has Morrigan's Magick and dip a finger into it. Now place that finger onto your third-eye chakra (in the middle of your forehead). With your eyes closed, summon me as a crow or raven. Connect with me through your third eye. With your eyes closed, look with your mind's eye. Do you see a crow or raven? The easiest way to tell is to look at the tail. Ravens have wedge-shaped tails, and crows have fan-shaped tails.

Once you have identified whether I have come to you as a crow or raven, sit back and accept the merging of energy. Men should be very wary of continuing at this point (again, unless you are a man with a lot of feminine energy). This energy merge will allow you to advance to the next part of transmutation with me as your guide. As you merge with the crow or raven, take special note of my feathers. They are much thicker than most humans realize.

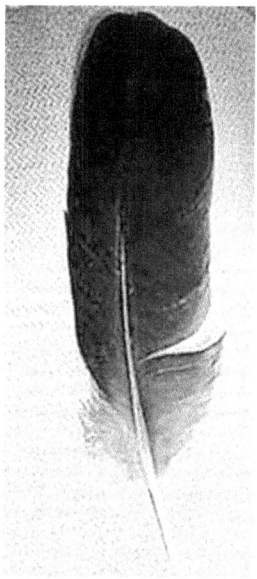

Crow Feather

As you merge with the crow or raven, your third eye may become cooler. Once you feel significantly merged, close the circle you have created by stating the following:

To the Witch of the West,
May your power depart
But your happiness and waters
Remain in my heart.

To the Witch of the South,
May your power depart
But your courage and fire
Remain in my heart.

To the Witch of the East,
May your power depart
But your clarity and air
Remain in my heart.

To the Witch of the North,
May your power depart
But your empathy and Earth
Remain in my heart.

To the Morrigan, the raven, and the crow energy,
Now I remember you, and you will remember me.
I close this circle but not my heart
Because this circle is only the start.
As this has always been, so mote it be.

I recommend waiting at least twenty-four hours until you attempt my next exercise in transmutation. Your consciousness will need to adapt to my energy.

It may not take everyone twenty-four hours to adapt, especially if you are someone who has received energy transfers or mergers before. Once you have adjusted, the next step is fairly easy. I recommend that this next step be done before going to bed or during a meditation when you have given yourself approximately an hour or two; it needs to be a very deep meditation. Before bed or before beginning your meditation, place a fingertip into Morrigan's Magick and place it on your third eye. Then recite the following:

> Now as (crow or raven), please take flight
> And guide my consciousness tonight.
> Together, we will find
> My totem with which I shall align.
> Our spirits will connect
> And when I wake, I shall recollect
> The journey we took and where we met
> And what was communicated at our tête-à-tête.

During this exercise, you will meet your animal totem. Take note of how large your totem is and where you met it. You will take this same route to meet your totem again. If your totem has wings, were you able to get on its back and fly? You may be surprised at how your animal totem looks in this particular dimension. If your totem is a bird, it might be as large as a horse. If your totem is a dragon, it might fill an entire cave. This spiritual meeting is going to allow you to merge your consciousness with your totem's in the next exercise.

Before explaining the next exercise, I would like to take this time to explain why I have chosen to guide you through transmutation with an animal. All animals are pure. While they kill, it is never for fun. It is for food. Animals do not receive joy or pleasure from bullying or putting another down. That is left to humans. Merging with your animal totem will allow your consciousness to experience a pure moment of transmutation. Also, animals do not fear death. It is a part of their cycle. Merging with your animal totem will allow you to understand why death should not be feared. It is your opportunity to reunite with your divine self and to continue on with the knowledge that you have gained from this most recent lifetime.

If you are having trouble with this exercise, and you have been unable to meet your totem, keep trying. You may not have been ready to meet your totem at this time. Another option is to email this transcriptionist and request that she program a rock and send it to you. When you receive the rock, dip it in Morrigan's Magick and place it under your pillow at night. Go through the above steps before falling asleep (stating the phrasing about meeting your totem).

Now, once you have made the pathway to your animal totem's location, the next step is to state the intention that you wish to merge your consciousness with that of your totem's. You do not have to begin this next step right away. You may wish to continue to meet with your totem and discuss what you wish with it. But when you are ready, place some Morrigan's Magick on your third eye. Make your intention known that you would like your animal totem to take your consciousness through transmutation and that you would like to then journey back to your human body. Everyone's experience with a totem will be unique, even for people who have the same totem. So I cannot tell you how you will feel or what you will experience. All I can do is assure you that I will be watching and making sure that your experience is positive.

Upon returning to your body, you will likely feel that your consciousness has been expanded and your frequency has been heightened. If you had any fears about transmutation before beginning, you will likely not have such feelings anymore. Those feelings have been transmuted and have been transformed into ones of comfort and peace. You will now be able to communicate with your animal totem whenever you like. You may call on your totem for strength when you need it.

Once you have a connection to the animal world, you should take note of any time that a particular animal crosses your path or comes into your dreams. You are likely receiving a message. For example, if a coyote crosses your path, the coyote may be telling you to be mindful of the risk-reward equation. Sometimes we need to play it safe, and other times, we need to take a clever leap of faith into something wholly new and challenging. It's likely that you are about to embark on a new situation, which calls for adaptation. Or perhaps you are seeing blue jays all of a sudden. The blue jay is spiritual, and it has been known to move between different spiritual worlds. Also, blue jays belong to the corvid family, which is the same as crows, magpies, ravens, rooks, jackdaws, treepies, choughs, and nutcrackers. So if you happen to see one of these birds quite regularly, you might just be getting a visit from me.

COMMENTARY BY ANUBIS

I want to thank The Morrigan, crow, and raven for their participation in this guide. If you have been blessed by crow or raven, you will know. Corvids display remarkable intelligence for animals of their size. They are among the most intelligent birds thus far studied. Did you know they are able to discern human faces? If you begin feeding crows or ravens, they will come to know you. And if you are someone who provides a negative experience to a crow or a raven, the community will know. They are able to communicate with one another and give guidance to others about which human was rude or mean. I would like to share another note to those reading this: Because The Morrigan has clearly made her stance known as it pertains to human men, if you have been harmed by one, you may wish to tell the crow or the raven. You might be surprised at what happens next.

Our next guide is Kali. Much like with The Morrigan, if you are a male, you may not wish to contact Kali. Kali is the Hindu goddess of ultimate power, time, destruction, and change. Kali is a supreme example of a powerful woman, who is self-confident and determined. She is not the stereotypical woman, who does as she's told. She is known for creation and destruction but also for her attachment to Shiva, her partner. Their relationship is strong. Each of them has a defined role to play. This feminism is one that sets up a woman as an equal partner to a man, and it is a strong one at that. There are no doubts in her mind or in Shiva's about who she is. This feminism does not demean anyone. Indeed, it gives everyone involved power. Significantly, Kali is feared by those who do not understand her and is revered by those who do. Which are you? It would be wise to be honest with yourself about your answer before choosing to proceed with Kali.

CHAPTER 4

KALI

I am so happy to introduce myself. I am Kali, the goddess of destruction and creation. This makes me perfect to assist with transmutation. We are going to transmute a space in the quantum field, which will be yours and yours alone. It is within this space that you will be able to begin to transmute your consciousness. This transmutation will take place as frequently as you wish once the space has been created.

While The Morrigan and I are geared more toward the divine feminine, for purposes of this guide, I strive to create a balance between the divine masculine and the divine feminine. So if you are male, you may certainly have me as your guide. But you must strive to maintain a balance between your masculine and feminine energies. I can also create a balance of the two by destroying abundance in either masculine or feminine energy and creating that balance. I am the goddess of creation and destruction for a reason. Before we get into energy transfers, destruction, and creation, I would like to cover one topic.

As with previous chapters, I am going to explain what my energy frequency is when combined with the number four. If you wish, you may tune into 444 hertz while reading this chapter. It may assist you in connecting with me. 444 hertz is called the master key because it is the one used to calibrate all the others. Many musical instruments are tuned to this frequency. It is said to kill cancer cells. It is an apparent carrier wave of love, broadcasting universally from the heart of the electromagnetic energetic matrix. It may help you align yourself with nature, bring a feeling of peace, and cause a pleasing sensation to the body and mind. You may wish to tune into this frequency while you connect with me. You may also wish to light a green candle (a beeswax candle if you have one). You may wish to focus on the flame during some of these exercises.

The first step to my process is understanding what you are. Humans—especially those who are connected to universal energies and frequencies—likely fit into one or more of the following categories: creator, destroyer, weaver, gatherer, protector, or lover. While they all have commonalities, each has very specific strengths. I am going to explain what each means and how each plays into the transmutation of space in the quantum field.

CREATORS

This seems pretty self-explanatory. Creators have the power to create. If you fit into this category, you are likely somewhat of a magician or manifester. This is more than just wishing for something and getting it. This has to do with creating something with your hands and mind. Some likely creators are musicians, artists, dancers, decorators, etc. You are able to think of something new like a piece of music or an item or clothing that has never been created before. You allow something to take over and execute the details of your idea flawlessly. Many creators are also likely to be destroyers.

DESTROYERS

This category is also self-explanatory. Creating and destroying go hand in hand, and they are the keys to transmutation. To create, you must destroy, and to destroy, you must create. What you destroy, you transmute into something new. When you create, you're transmuting energy or an actual object into something new. For example, you are a designer, and you are creating a new dress. The fabric you are using to create something new is being destroyed from what it was before. On a larger scale, to create a planet, an interstellar cloud collapses out of a nebula, thus destroying the previous energy of that interstellar cloud. Now, if you are more of a destroyer than a creator and you either do not or have not understood your gift, you likely have some issues with depression. Wanting to break down something like a relationship or a structure and then seeing it happen is a lot to take on for most humans. The key is to understand that when you destroy something, you are able to transmute it into something else. In most cases, humans just see the destruction and become depressed at the revelation that their desire for this destruction is why it happened. This can bring about many negative feelings, which allow negative energies into your space. You are then susceptible to using your gift for a negative force, and you may have issues with feeling like you are being possessed by a negative force. By understanding your gift, however, you are actually able to destroy even those negative energies and transmute them into a different space or dimension.

WEAVERS

Weavers are interesting. They are able to fit into every category because of their ability to weave spells or the energy to create, destroy, gather, protect, and love. The transcriptionist is a weaver; she is weaving this book at this very second. I call them weavers because what they do is like the web of a spider. Weavers innately know how to connect ideas and energy. They are able to do so in the order that something must be accomplished. Weavers seem to get through life easily. It is because of this gift that they are able to do so. If they want something to happen, they are able to manifest their thoughts by creating something of a web with their gift. They know the words that need to be said and have the energy to connect with those words. Sometimes there is an action that must be taken, which they are also innately aware of. The danger for weavers is that if they do not know of their gift, they could interfere with fate. Interfering with fate has dangerous consequences. So within a weave, the weaver must always interject the energy or the thought that while they want a weave to work, they also must not interfere with fate and do not want to manifest something that would do so.

GATHERERS

Most gatherers are nurturers. These humans innately know the ingredients that are needed for anything—a fabulous party, recipe, spell, prayer, etc. Many gatherers are also creators. Gatherers are sensitive humans (sensitive in the manner that they get their feelings hurt often). They feel emotions much more so than other humans do, so most gatherers are likely empaths. Because of a gatherer's ability to feel so intensely and to connect with others so easily, some gatherers are susceptible to addiction. This is so because if a gatherer does not want his or her gift of being empathic, he or she may attempt to block feelings by drinking alcohol or picking up other addictive behaviors. As with destroyers, the key is to understand your gift. Another key is understanding how to create a block to other energies when you do not wish to feel them so intensely. (As I said, many gatherers are also creators.) To create a block, all you need to do is gather some positive energy with your crown or third-eye chakra and spread it around yourself like a shield or a force field. When you want to disperse the shield, just clap your hands three times—the sound will break up the energy—and state, "I command this energy to disperse."

PROTECTORS

Protectors are so important, but many individuals who are protectors do not actually know they are. This is because they are likely to enter the law-enforcement field. And those who are in the law-enforcement field are not likely to open themselves up to intuition or thoughts of the beyond. Protectors are good to have in covens. Although part of a coven's ritual is to form a boundary, beyond which, nothing but the things that have been called may pass, a protector seals that boundary with something like steel. No one is able to pass through without the protector's approval. Protectors are also important to have during a time when someone may be experimenting with a Ouija board. Protectors innately know how to form a protective barrier. They also serve as the gatekeeper—an energy that does not let anything other than high-frequency light energy pass through it. While most humans must request a gatekeeper from the other side, protectors do not need to do so. But again, protectors are hard to come by. These humans are the most likely to reject their potential of being able to know what is on the other side of the veil.

LOVERS

This is a newer category, which I have created. This category came to me because of the repatterning of Earth. At around 2020, humans in this category may have started feeling the opening of their heart chakra much more than before. What is interesting about lovers is that weavers and creators (either knowingly or not) had a part in creating this category. People had some time on their hands in 2020, and through their thoughts and abilities to manifest, weavers and creators assisted the human race by shifting the patterns of others and pinpointing those who would be open to a heart-chakra transmutation. If you are a lover, your bonds with other people may have begun strengthening in 2020 also. Lovers are tuned in to relationships. They make decisions based on what they feel their heart chakra is telling them to do. Like gatherers, they are very sensitive and likely to be empaths. They have become necessary for the human race. Lovers innately bring joy to other people's lives. They are able to open another person's heart chakra by focusing on their own heart-chakra's energy and transferring that energy to the other person's. It is really quite remarkable how this category came to be. Through lovers, the human race was given hope during a time that many of you believed was negative.

Some humans may not know whether they fit into any specific category. I am happy to complete an energy transfer for those who would like this knowledge. For those of you who already know which category (or categories) you are in, you may still receive this energy transfer if you would like. All you need to do is sit quietly. Make sure the soles of your feet are firmly planted on the ground and no limbs are crossed. You may set the palms of your hands on your knees if you would like. Now, breathe in and out through your nose. Breathe in for six counts, hold it for six counts, and then breathe out for six counts. Repeat this process three times. Imagine me sitting across from you. My eyes are closed. You may also close yours if you wish. My energy transfer will come through my eyes. So when you see my eyes open, you will begin receiving the transfer. The transfer will come from my eyes to yours. If you are a creator, you will see a grain of sand. If you are a destroyer, you will see a skull within the top portion of an X. Weavers will see a spider or a web. Gatherers will see a broom, and protectors will see a hammer. Lovers will see either a heart or the Earth. Remember, you may see more than one symbol because some people are in more than one category. If you see something else, you are not in any one of these categories. But remember what you see because you will need this when we create your space within the quantum field. You will use it to begin creating your space and calling on me for assistance.

Before we begin creating your transmutation space within the quantum field, I would first like to touch on the topic of death. So many humans doubt there is something beyond the life they are currently living. People like to quote Karl Marx by saying that religion is the opium of the people. Atheists hold this sentence close to their hearts, and in turn, they lead very closed-off lives. I would like to counter Marx's thought by saying what if all there is after this life is what you imagine it to be? What if your thoughts are the things that manifest what you will be and experience after this life? Those who believe that they are snuffed out after this life are actually snuffed out because it is the afterlife that they have created for themselves. I love to laugh at those humans because they are those who typically do nothing for their fellow humans and therefore, do not leave their mark. They are not remembered for anything. They are forgotten. What if by creating the space where you will go after your human form has completed its journey in this lifetime, you ensure that your consciousness will transmute safely and peacefully and that your consciousness will continue beyond the human form you are currently inhabiting? That is what you will get with me as your guide: a guarantee.

There are two keys to transmutation. The first is this: To create, you must destroy, and to destroy, you must create. It seems pretty simple, but it is also one of those keys that sometimes you don't realize until it is stated. So when you create something, you are destroying something else and vice versa. It's a little bit like a math equation: creation + destruction = transmutation and destruction + creation = transmutation. The second key is that you must equally love what you are creating and what you are destroying. This makes sense when you apply this logic to death. The death of your human form creates your pure spirit form. I think the difficult part for some of you will be that you need to love your human form as much as you love your spirit form. Self-hatred among humans seems rampant. For some, it is easy to love others but loving yourself is not only difficult but also almost impossible. So I am going to assist you with that. I am going to transmute that self-hatred into self-love.

By living in duality, humans are faced with a blessing and a curse. By experiencing and knowing what you consider dark or negative forces and feelings, you are able to truly know the light and positive forces and feelings. It may be said that only by experiencing the dark does a person get to know the light. Unfortunately, some humans have difficultly escaping dark or negative thoughts about themselves—feelings and thoughts like, *I am lazy, I am ugly, I am fat,* and *Everyone would be better off without me.* Additionally, other humans get pleasure out of hurting others. This can take the form of an abusive friendship, romantic relationship, familial relationship, etc. This, in turn, has lasting effects on the human psyche. So many humans feel unworthy of love, so much so, that they do not love themselves. Some humans turn to addictive behaviors and practices as a way of coping with past hurts. But these behaviors do not allow a human to heal and move on. They actually make you more depressed.

Before explaining and conducting a healing exercise, I want to touch on the topic of consuming sadness. The practice that humans engage in when dealing with the meat industry is extremely harmful. Some humans breed animals for the sole purpose of killing those animals. These humans do not give animals enough credit for their emotional intelligence. Animals are extremely adept at receiving understanding through their emotions. Not all humans engage in this practice. Indeed, as previously stated, I am a Hindu goddess. The respect for animal rights in Jainism, Hinduism, and Buddhism derives from the doctrine of *ahimsa*. Ahimsa is an ancient Indian principle of nonviolence, which applies to all living beings. It is a key virtue in the Indian religions of Jainism, Buddhism, Hinduism, and Sikhism. Ahimsa is a multidimensional concept, which is inspired by the premise that all living beings have a spark of divine spiritual energy; therefore, to hurt another being is to hurt oneself. Ahimsa has also been related to the notion that any violence has karmic consequences. Perhaps the most popular advocate of the principle of ahimsa in modern times was Mahatma Gandhi.[4]

In Hinduism, animals contain a soul just like humans do. These beliefs have resulted in many Hindus practicing vegetarianism. Jain doctrine mandates vegetarianism based on its strict interpretation of the doctrine of ahimsa. Mahayana Buddhists similarly practice vegetarianism and prohibit the killing of animals. In Hinduism, many animals are venerated, including the tiger, elephant, mouse, and especially, the cow. Mahayana Buddhism teaches that "we can only escape our own suffering if we avoid inflicting it on others."[5]

---

[4] Gandhi, M., *The Essential Gandhi: An Anthology of His Writings on His Life, Work, and Ideas* (Random House Digital, Inc., 2000).
[5] Grant, Catharine, "The No-Nonsense Guide to Animal Rights," *New Internationalist* (2006), 22–26.

Breeding animals for the sole purpose of killing and consuming them is actually harmful to humans and their consciousness. When these animals are born, they know and understand why they are alive. Not only do they understand that they are going to die unnaturally but also that they are given harmful chemicals by humans. Can you imagine this type of existence? Women are likely to connect with this more than men will because women are much more intuitive and empathic. These emotions are felt throughout those animals' bodies. They feel a constant surge of depression, frustration, anger, etc. Then once they are killed, packaged, and distributed, humans eat their limbs. They are consuming sadness and depression. This does not help the human body rid itself of negative emotions. Instead, it fuels the cells with it. The next time you decide to consume packaged meat, look up an image of a meat farm while you are consuming it.

There was a recorded story about a cow crying. Please feel free to research this. The story is about a cow that had been saved by an animal sanctuary. The cow believed she was on her way to getting slaughtered. A photographer captured her crying. This showed that she was able to feel emotions—particularly sadness and fear.

I encourage you to think about this story the next time you are consuming packaged meat. Again, you're not just consuming the meat but also consuming the feelings of those animals, which know they were bred just to die an unnatural death. So your cells aren't only receiving protein but also sadness, depression, anger, etc. You are consuming sadness. This type of consumption will not help you when you're trying to raise your frequency.

Let's now begin your journey into the quantum field. I will assist you in getting to your space where you will construct your transmutation location. For my assistance and an energy transfer, just say my name four times (since we are focusing on the number four). You may see me next to you or my consciousness or energy connecting with your space. I give the gift of balance. You must be balanced to have a safe and effortless journey into transmutation. I hold the secret to the balance of male and female energy. When you feel balanced, allow your consciousness to enter into the quantum field. I will give you coordinates so that you may find your transmutation location easily the next time you want to journey there. The coordinates are essentially latitude and longitude numbers. Because the human mind is generally focused on maps and spaces, it seems the best way to communicate your transmutation location. Because the quantum field is endless and infinite, no one will have the same location coordinates. If you are unable to see or hear your coordinates, just contact the transcriptionist and request that she channel me to send you your location coordinates.

The manner in which you construct your space will depend on your category—creator, destroyer, weaver, gatherer, protector, or lover. If you are not sure which category you belong to, I will assist you in creating your space because I am the ultimate force of creation and destruction. If you know which category you belong to, this is how you will continue:

Category	Creator	Destroyer	Weaver	Gatherer	Protector	Lover
How to Begin	Focus on a grain of sand.	Focus on a bright star.	Create a web.	Think of a basketful of endless energy orbs.	Think of a force field.	Focus on your heart chakra.

If you are not sure what category you are in, think of a circle. And if you belong to more than one category, begin with the category that you feel has the strongest pull on you. Now begin to build your transmutation location as follows.

CREATORS

Use that grain of sand and multiply it. Watch the grains turn into whatever you like. Perhaps they turn into colors, trees, grass, plants, or a particular room. It's whatever you would like to have in the space that your consciousness will be traveling to. You might want a grain of sand to turn into a magick wand. Then you may allow this wand to draw and create whatever you like in your space. It is that easy. The quantum field is yours to create your own reality. At this point, I would just advise against creating sentient beings in your space. Perhaps there will be another book where I will explain how to do that and about the care you must continue to give to these beings. This is my cautionary instruction to you creators. If you would like further instruction, I advise you to contact the transcriptionist and request that I be channeled for additional instructions regarding your creating of sentient beings within your transmutation location.

DESTROYERS

As I previously mentioned, destroyers are also likely creators because to create, you must destroy, and to destroy, you must create. But if you feel pulled more toward being a destroyer, focus on a star. The star you focus on within your location must be massive. When a massive star dies, there's enough gravitational pressure to not only fuse hydrogen but also helium, carbon, oxygen, magnesium, and silicon. A good number of the elements on the periodic table is produced inside a giant star near the end of its life. Now imagine your giant star forming an iron core. Think of the core contracting until it turns the entire core into a giant ball of neutrons. That neutron ball is able to resist the crushing collapse and triggers a supernova blast. A supernova will release more energy in a week than our sun releases over the course of its entire ten-billion-year lifetime. Once you have imagined that blast occurring, you will transmute that energy into what you want included in your transmutation location. All categories will receive this same cautionary instruction: Do not transmute that energy into sentient beings. If you would like to learn what is involved with that type of transmutation, contact the transcriptionist and request that she channel me to create a guide with this type of instruction.

WEAVERS

You are going to weave what you like into your space. First, think of what you would like for your initial weave. Perhaps it is a pillow, a bed, a cloud, or your favorite sweater. Start with something small. Now imagine your hand. With your index finger, begin creating a web for this object. Perhaps within the web are words or a chant. (Within this web that I create shall be the pillow that I meet upon my fate.) You can use anything you wish to line the web—musical notes, words, colors, geometrical shapes, formulas, emotions, etc. What you are placing in your space will be formed within the cocoon of your web. Once you have finished creating your cocoon, you may watch the object form within it. When it is complete, you will see the object absorb the cocoon. Continue adding to your transmutation location throughout your life. This is where you will initially advance to once your human body has served its purpose on Earth. You have the same cautionary instruction: Do not create any sentient beings.

GATHERERS

At your location, you will find a basketful of infinite energy orbs. Think of what you would like to initially include within your space. As with the weavers, it might be best to start small—a broom, pillow, stuffed animal, flower, etc. Think of what you would like and pick an energy orb from the basket. Hold it in your hands and state, "I am gathering _____ [a structure, a tree, a floor plan, etc.] for transmutation location _____ and _____ [your location coordinates] within the quantum field." You will be able to watch the energy orb transmute into the object. As you move into gathering larger structures (a home, floor plan, fully grown tree, etc.), you will follow the steps described and then release the orb. You will be able to watch your structure form from the energy orb. Again, you have the same cautionary instruction: Do not gather sentient beings. Until you are skilled and understand what's involved with gathering a sentient being, do not do so.

PROTECTORS

Since I am also a protective energy, protectors will be calling on me to assist them with their transmutation location. As I stated, you are going to create a force field around your location. Transfuse something personal around it—your initials, a picture, or a hologram of your favorite toy when you were a child (or your current favorite toy). This will assist you in finding your location without any trouble, anytime you want to return. To bring the items you want into your space, you're going to ask me to create them. You will do this by taking a piece of paper and writing the following:

> Kali, goddess of creation and goddess of time,
> I ask you to bring _____ into this space of mine.
> Thank you for your help. Thank you for your energy.
> As I ask, so mote it be.

Do this for any item that you would like. You may also insert a picture. I will create any object or structure that you want. I do not need to provide you with a cautionary instruction because I will not bring any sentient beings into your space (unless another guide is written to explain how you should take care of them).

LOVERS

Since I am also the goddess of creation, I am going to assist you in the creation of your transmutation location. Whenever you would like to begin, just say, "Kali, please come to _____ and _____ [location coordinates] and assist me in creating my transmutation location." You're going to create your space through love. For you, each item will begin with a thought and then a feeling. First, think about your first object. As with the other categories, it would be best to start small. For anything you think of, surround that object with love. If you would like it to be in your transmutation location, you likely have an emotional connection to it. Imagine that object within your heart chakra. Surround it with love and light. Once you have materialized the object within your heart chakra, I will pull it out and place it within your space. You will continue this until you have completed your space. As with the protectors, I do not need to provide you with a cautionary instruction because I will not bring any sentient beings into your space (unless another guide is written to explain how you should take care of them).

FREQUENCY 444

This category is for those who do not know which category they fit into, but they would like to create their transmutation location. Your process will be much like the protectors, except you will begin with a circle. which I will transmute into a force field. Transfuse something personal around it—your initials, a picture, a hologram of your favorite toy when you were a child, or your current favorite toy. This will assist you in finding your location without any trouble, anytime you want to return. To call on me to transmute your circle into a force field, just state, "Kali, please come to _____ and _____ [your coordinates] in the quantum field and help me transmute my circle into a force field." To bring the items you want into your space, you're going to ask me to create each one. You will do this by taking a piece of paper and writing the following:

> Kali, goddess of creation and time,
> I ask you to bring _____ into this space of mine.
> Thank you for your help. Thank you for your energy.
> As I ask, so mote it be.

Do this for any item that you would like. You may also insert a picture. I will create any object or structure you would like. As with protectors and lovers, I do not need to provide you with a cautionary instruction because I will not bring any sentient beings into your space (unless another guide is written to explain how you should take care of them).

Continue to create your transmutation location as much as you like. The more you visit, the less confused you will be at the time of transmutation. Because you know where you are going, you will know what to expect. Before we finish, I want to explain why it is important not to create sentient beings within your transmutation location. If the being you want to create already exists, you would essentially be creating a clone. Also, have you ever read the book *Pet Sematary* by Stephen King? When you do not know how to go about creating a sentient being, there is a chance that something could go very wrong. So for the purposes of this book and exercise, if there is someone whom you wish to be there upon your transmutation, create, weave, gather, or request that a doll be made in that person's image. This way, the message will get to that individual that you would like him or her to be there in your transmutation location and to greet you. Also, I will be waiting there—either at the moment of transmutation to help guide you or at your transmutation location. The more you connect with me, the easier it will be.

So what do I look like? It's important to remember that that you will be connecting with my energy. But I also know that as humans, you like to connect a name with a particular form. I also know that almost all of you have likely looked me up on the internet and have had various thoughts and emotions about those forms that I have taken. For some of you, my blue form (coming with my many arms and my tongue sticking out) is comforting. This might be because you connect with my warrior form or understand that the more formidable that I look, the more I am able to protect. But the important thing for you is to connect with my energy. Once you have connected with my energy, you may picture my image more like Green Tara's if you would like. Or you may wish to see me in my traditional form. Some of you consider that form to be frightening, which is why some of you may wish to see me in a form that is more akin to Green Tara's.

Thank you for allowing me to be your guide. I am looking forward to working with so many of you. And remember, if you would like an additional guide to be made (regarding the creating of sentient beings), contact the transcriptionist. I would love to share this knowledge with you. Namaste.

COMMENTARY BY ANUBIS

Thank you, Kali. I know that anyone who chooses to work with Kali will gain so much knowledge from her. She is rather close to the transcriptionist. So the transcriptionist works with Kali almost on a daily basis. This is because Kali gave some of her energy to the creation of this transcriptionist's consciousness. Anyone who chooses to work with Kali will likely be drawn to her because of Kali giving some of her energy to this person's consciousness.

The next chapter is Aphrodite. I have worked with Aphrodite on a number of occasions. Transmutation and love are closely interwoven. I encourage everyone reading this book to go through the chapter with Aphrodite. She is going to teach and explain how to connect with your higher self. This will allow you to learn how to love and forgive yourself. So many humans have a difficult time with transmutation because they have so many unresolved issues. Aphrodite is going to give you guidance on how to work through those issues, especially when you are unable to connect with the human who has wronged you or whom you have wronged. Aphrodite and Kuan Yin have similar messages. So it might be beneficial to you to read both chapters. They are interwoven and both contain messages of forgiveness, love, and mercy.

CHAPTER 5

APHRODITE

I would like to begin by thanking you for inviting me into your life. To those of you who chose or saw the number five during Anubis's introduction, you are very special to me. The number five is related to personal freedom, independence, individualism, adaptability, major life changes, and life lessons learned through experience. It also symbolizes motivation, determination, adventure, courage, imagination, and making positive choices. Because the body has a head and four limbs, five fingers on each hand, and five toes on each foot and because we have five senses, five is the number of humanity. Indeed, our five fingers and toes are often the very definition of our humanness—all are checked fervently at birth.

There is something inherently special in the number five. Its geometric shape—the five-pointed star—is globally recognized as the mark of excellence. Movies, restaurants, and hotels are all graded by the number of stars they are given (with five being the highest).

Those who associate with the number five and its energies or who have a life path directed by the number five are known to be free-spirited but modest. They are self-sufficient, vivacious, curious, and quick to act. They recognize the beauty in so much and likely strive to make their living environments perfectly beautiful.

In the Tarot, the five is associated with the Hierophant. The Hierophant is the masculine counterpart to the High Priestess. This does not mean that only men may be Hierophants; it just means that women who are Hierophants are likely to have some masculine energy. The Hierophant is the card of traditional values and institutions. The Hierophant can represent a counselor or mentor who will provide you with wisdom and guidance or a spiritual or religious advisor such as a priest, vicar, preacher, imam, rabbi, or a monk. Alternatively, it can represent someone who is very set in their ways.

My frequency, when combined with the number five, is 888 hertz. Music at 888 hertz symbolizes miracles, opening up the abundance gate, and connecting with the angelic realms. This number is sacred in many cultures, religions, and spiritual traditions. It symbolizes completion, good luck, and perfect balance. It also represents the planetary star Merkaba, which offers the energy of unconditional love and enlightenment. The Merkaba is an ancient shape constructed using two tetrahedrons. Each spins opposite of the other, creating a three-dimensional field of energy.

Merkaba

Merkaba means light, spirit, and body. It is the energy sphere where everything exists. It is the vehicle that carries you to the dimensions of unity and love, which exist beyond the mind.

While Archangel Metatron is associated with the Merkaba, they are lending this symbol and its power to me for the purpose of assisting you in connecting with your higher self. Before proceeding, I want to give a little background on Archangel Metatron. Archangel Metatron is the Archangel of Empowerment. They are one of only two angels (along with Sandalphon) that are believed to have ascended from a human incarnation on Earth and into the angelic realm.[6] Metatron is revered as one of the most powerful Archangels, as they represent our ability to access spiritual power and achieve ascension.

Metatron has historically used Sacred Geometry in the form of a Merkaba Cube, which may be used by you for the purpose of forgiving yourself and healing from past emotional wounds. As I indicated earlier, it will also serve as a personal portal to your higher self. Archangel Metatron may present themselves to you during your journey in this chapter and assist you (along with myself) in connecting with your higher self. They presented themselves to the transcriptionist when she learned how to merge with her higher self.

Because the phrase "Sacred Geometry" was mentioned, I want to explain a little about what it means. Sacred geometry ascribes symbolic and sacred meanings to certain geometric shapes and proportions. Sacred geometry symbols are known as ancient shapes and patterns, which are believed to represent all living things. These symbols are regarded as the most perfect and divine shapes because they are regarded as the blueprints of many life-forms in the universe. Also dubbed as the language of the gods, these sacred symbols are a depiction of everything that is mystical and abstract in this world. According to Sacred Geometry, patterns in nature are viewed from a mathematical viewpoint, and they have broad implications. The sacred part is a belief that these patterns, their mathematical formulas, and their structures are evidence of divine planning and creation.

---

[6] Enoch, the biblical prophet and scribe, is believed to be the human incarnation of Metatron. Once ascended, Metatron was given the all-important task of writing down all choices made in heaven and on Earth in a universal archive referred to as the Book of Life or the Akashic record.

The spiral of a snail's shell, the pattern of a single snowflake, and the branches of a tree are all examples of sacred geometry. Sacred geometry is also thought to exist beyond the naked eye, both on a cellular level and in the stars and on orbiting planets. In terms of sacred geometry, the Merkaba consists of thirteen circles, which are connected by straight lines. The resultant pattern looks like two stars embedded in a hexagon. It contains all geometric shapes in the Universe, and it is believed to be a geometric map for the Universe. It also contains the platonic solids, which are said to be the fundamental elements of all physical matter.[7] From crystals to DNA, these forms can be found everywhere in existence. Within its center, you can also see the Egg of Life.[8] Metatron's Cube is considered to be the guardian of the universe.

Because there are many sacred geometric symbols, if you do not feel connected to the Merkaba, please feel free to research and find another form of sacred geometry to connect with. You may feel a greater energetic pull to the Flower of Life, the Seed of Life, or perhaps a different symbol.

Beyond the Merkaba, another example of sacred geometry is the Flower of Life. This symbol contains all necessary information about every

---

[7] The platonic solids are three-dimensional shapes with faces that are of equal size. An example of a platonic solid is the great pyramid of ancient Egypt, which has four identical faces. There are five platonic solids: tetrahedron (four faces in a pyramid shape), hexahedron (six6 faces in a cube), octahedron (eight faces), dodecahedron (twelve faces), and icosahedron (twenty faces). These platonic solids were identified by Plato. The ancient Greeks use these five shapes to represent earth, fire, air, water, and spirit.

[8] In sacred geometry, it is the second iteration while forming the Flower of Life. As such, it has about thirteen circles.

Flower of Life

Egg of Life

living thing in this world. Moreover, it depicts the interconnectedness of all life-forms. The Flower of Life has seven overlapping symmetrical circles, which are in the shape of a flower. Many people believe that this formation represents the growth of a tree—from growing roots to bearing fruits.

Flower of Life

Another sacred geometric symbol is the Seed of Life. The Seed of Life is a universal symbol of creation. It is found at the heart of the Flower of Life and it has an entire cosmology of consciousness encoded into its singular geometric seed.

Seed of Life

The Seed of Life is formed from a relationship of six circles around one, equaling seven circles). Each circle fits into this pattern like a lock and key, forms a dynamic field of possible geometric relationships, and reveals the most fundamental shapes of creation. These seven circles mirror our chakras, the colors of the rainbow, and even musical scales. They form a foundation upon which the infinite nature of life can be understood.

The Hamsa Hand is a very popular geometric shape, which is synonymous with Middle Eastern traditions and cultures. There are two common variants: two symmetrical thumbs at each corner of the hand or a single thumb. Hamsa represents the hand of the creator of all life-forms. In Middle Eastern tradition, Hamsa brings good health, good luck, prosperity, and joy. In the Hebrew culture, all five fingers of the Hamsa Hand depict the five books contained in the Torah.

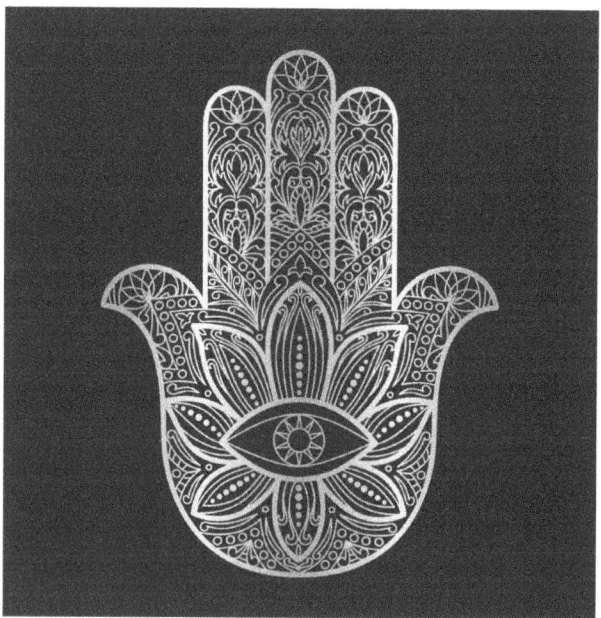

Hamsa

I am going to give you one more example of a sacred geometric symbol, which many of you will connect with: the Eternal Knot.

Eternal Knot

The Eternal Knot, also known as the Endless Knot or Tibetan Knot, is one of the eight auspicious symbols in Buddhism. The others are the Treasure Vase, Victory Banner, Pair of Golden Fish, Parasol, Lotus, and Conch Shell. While the knot is a typical Buddhist element, it is also found in ancient Chinese culture. It also bears resemblance to some ancient Celtic Knots. Its shape is an elaborate, infinite design of looped lines at ninety-degree angles. It represents the eternal cycle of life, death, and rebirth, time, and the quest for spiritual growth.

Other famous examples include Buddhist Mandalas or Leonardo da Vinci's *Vitruvian Man*. Even the *Mona Lisa* is said to be painted with sacred geometric patterns underlying it. The golden ratio can be found in Mozart's music and the Fibonacci sequence in Egyptian pyramids. Symbolically, the Fibonacci sequence is representative of the chakras, which are turning in circles, forming a spiral energy vortex, and igniting kundalini energy. It can also form the basis of a labyrinth, which is another important spiritual, sacred geometry shape—the pilgrimage to spiritual enlightenment. These shapes are said to be the metaphysical language that governs the visible and invisible world.

It is important to cover this information because I am going to activate a form of sacred geometry within you. You will use it to connect to your higher self. You may want to craft your own sacred geometrical symbol. It could be a combination of the symbols that are already considered sacred. You may wish to draw something yourself, which you feel will geometrically represent your connection to your higher self.

Before we begin, I would like to provide you with some background about your higher self and the import of connecting with your higher self. Your higher self is your soul consciousness; it's unlimited and eternal. Connecting with your higher self is a paradox. You are always connected. It's more than a connection. It's unity. The catch is knowing how to recognize that connection and channel the answers that you seek to your human brain. Because you will be reuniting with your higher self when your human consciousness transmutes, recognizing your higher self is important. While your physical self is your current life (i.e., your human personality), your higher self is your multi-life (i.e., spirit personality). Connecting with your higher self gives you an ability to connect directly to your past lives and spirit guides. The following benefits are just some that come from connecting with your higher self:

- Your life is meaningful no matter what's happening in your life.
- You have a greater purpose, and your life events have a purpose.
- You perceive suffering as your opportunity to learn and grow.
- You are empowered, and you're cocreating with life.
- Your life feels magical.
- You feel supported and connected.

I know that Xia covered past lives and how to connect with them in a different way. I am giving you an alternative way. Also, I want to provide a note regarding past lives. It can be jarring to suddenly realize that there have been many "yous" and that some of your forms were not human. Take a minute to reflect and internalize those thoughts and feelings. Before connecting with your higher self, think about who you could have been in a past life. Perhaps you were a different sex or in a form that was androgynous. (Many alien forms are androgynous.) Try becoming comfortable with having different forms from the one you inhabit today. You have likely been through tremendous strife—the universe is timeless. And your consciousness is in human form to learn some very important lessons. Some of those lessons are how to overcome very difficult obstacles. Some of those obstacles include living with a physical issue (for example, the transcriptionist lived a human life as a conjoined twin), living a life in extreme poverty, etc. But through these lives, you have experienced and learned valuable lessons that you impart into the universe. When you connect to your higher self, you will be able to absorb those lessons and gifts that you obtained while you lived through strife, poverty, etc.

Now you are going to connect with me. My frequency is extremely high, and it may be difficult for some of you to feel or connect with. I recommend searching for a channel that plays the 888-hertz frequency. I also recommend that while playing that music in the background, you take a bowl and fill it with water. I am associated with the following symbols: the dolphin, rose, scallop shell, myrtle, dove, sparrow, and swan. Look into the bowl of water and see which of my symbols you think about first. Once it comes to mind, stare into the water a little longer. Then close your eyes. Keep my symbol in your mind, breathe, and focus. The symbols may turn into the shape of my human form, or it may stay a symbol. It does not matter. What matters is that through the symbol, you find my frequency. There will be no doubt when it happens. You will feel a sense of calm, peace, and love. Focus on that feeling.

Next, I, in either the form of my symbol or my human form, will appear in front of you with a symbol of sacred geometry in my hands. Focus on that symbol. Is it the Merkaba? (Many of you will see the Merkaba.) Perhaps it's the Flower of Life. Do you see it spinning? What color is it? Or is it more than one color? Continue to focus on the symbol for as long as it takes you to become comfortable with it. Sacred geometry symbols hold so much magick.

In this next step, I will be placing the sacred geometry symbol in your heart chakra, where I will then activate it. You may wait if you wish before continuing onto this next step. While my energy is soft and subtle, the awakening of a sacred geometry symbol in your heart chakra will feel differently for everyone. To ensure that this is done freely, please state the following three times: "Aphrodite, please activate _____ [name of sacred geometric symbol] in my heart chakra." Wait a few minutes after making this statement so that the symbol may incorporate itself into your consciousness. You will use this to connect with your higher self. Unless you are used to energy transfers, I recommend waiting at least twenty-four hours until you proceed to the next step. You may certainly read the next step to prepare yourself, but actually doing the next step should not happen immediately. Allow your consciousness to acclimate to your increased frequency.

The next step is connecting with your higher self. To connect with your higher self, begin by focusing on the sacred geometric symbol that has been activated in your heart chakra. It should begin to spin once you focus on it. Now, state your purpose: "I am activating _____ [name of sacred geometric symbol] to connect with my higher self." You will see a strand of light extending up and down. That strand of light is going to extend through your crown and root chakras. It will infinitely extend up and down. As it extends upward through your crown chakra, it will begin turning clockwise. Once it begins turning clockwise, it will begin to expand. Its expansion will continue little by little until it surrounds you. Take a minute to note how you feel. Many will feel energy coming through the palms of your hands and the soles of your feet. Allow the expansion to take place and note the color of the energy you are seeing. Most of you will see gold or white. Some of you will feel energy in your throat chakra. (This is because your higher self is beginning to communicate with you.) For those who may not feel this connection, don't worry. Just try again and ask me to help you with establishing this connection.

When you are comfortable, ask your higher self some questions. Ask your higher self to show you your most recent past life, or perhaps you want to know what you have come to Earth to learn or to teach to others. Some of you may not be reaching your full potential. Why is that? Is it self-doubt? Fear and doubt are consequences of the human ego. Your higher self helps to free you from this constraint. In connecting with your higher self, you will feel what it is like to be free from ego and therefore, free of doubt, fear, etc. It is very likely that many reading this have told themselves that their thoughts or ideas are not good enough or that an idea that they have had is stupid. I assure you that it is not. Your human ego constrains your ability to practice spirituality. The transcriptionist has thought about creating this guide for years, but she did not begin creating this guide until she was able to free herself of her human ego. So many humans doubt their abilities (especially when it comes to spirituality). How many times have you had a strong intuitive feeling about something, but then you convinced yourself that your intuition was wrong or stupid? That is your ego at work. Connecting with your higher self will allow you to begin understanding what it feels like not to have those doubts about yourself.

When you ask your higher self questions, recognize how your higher self answers. Some of you may hear a voice. Others may receive images. And others may receive an answer in the form of a feeling. There are many ways you may communicate with your higher self. The key is fine-tuning and practicing your ability to hear those messages.

As stated earlier, another benefit of connecting with your higher self is understanding how to forgive yourself. Perhaps there is one (or quite a few) choice or choices that you have made, which you have asked yourself, *Why did I do that? I wish I had never done that.* Perhaps that choice caused significant trauma to you and others. Having these thoughts and reliving that choice perpetuates the negative feelings that come with it. You carry that emotional baggage around with you because you have not forgiven yourself. This baggage causes some not to be able to enter transmutation easily. This type of baggage may also cause transmutation to end with your consciousness just exiting your human body and not continuing onward. There is no benefit to you or the universe in that.

While connecting with your higher self, you will be able to learn how to forgive yourself and move on from that event. Please note that forgiving another person for what he or she has done to you is part of the next chapter with Kuan Yin. This chapter is about forgiving yourself. There may be a reason why you were fated to make that choice. Perhaps you made a similar choice in a past life, and your consciousness from that life is still on Earth. By forgiving yourself in this lifetime, your consciousness from your past lifetime (and this lifetime) will be able to meet with your higher self upon transmutation. Have that conversation with your higher self. Because your higher self exists without ego, you will be able to feel how to move on and forgive yourself. Given that you are human, however, you may need to have that conversation with your higher self more than once. Some humans seem to enjoy ruminating on choices that have gone wrong. I have never understood why they do this. Do you enjoy feeling bad about yourself? Or perhaps you're so used to feeling negatively about yourself that you don't know how to exist without feeling that way. Whatever the reason, you must choose not to feel that way about yourself. Although your higher self will consistently give you the same clarity time and again, why would you need clarity more than once? Moving on without feeling badly about yourself must also be a choice.

You may also ask for my assistance by focusing on your sacred geometric symbol within your heart chakra and ask for my help. Loving yourself takes practice. It is one of the hardest things for humans to do. Even narcissistic humans, who love what they look like on the outside, but on the inside, they are insecure and have many doubts that they can be loved. Truly loving yourself is exhibited by extending kindness and love toward others. I understand, though, that it is difficult not to feel things like jealousy or impatience. That's OK. The point is for you to recognize that you are feeling that way and to know how to evaluate and dissipate that emotion.

Because I am the goddess of love and beauty, I am going to take the next page or so to discuss the standard of beauty in society and the way to get past that and to love yourself how you are. This does not mean disregarding health warnings from doctors. (Making sure that your heart and body are healthy is key.) This just means that having plastic surgery done just to please someone else is unnecessary. It is time to understand that there is beauty in being different. You chose the body you would come to Earth in. It was your choice to have a nose that is perhaps a little bigger than average. It was your choice to be shorter or taller than average. Connecting with your higher self will allow you to begin loving and accepting yourself the way you are.

Beauty standards have changed throughout human history. Did you know that during the Middle Ages, women plucked their foreheads? A high forehead was considered beautiful. So if a woman did not have a naturally high forehead, she raised her hairline artificially. Up until the early twentieth century, pale skin was much desired by European ladies of standing. Being pale was a status symbol; it told the world that you did not have to work outside. Instead, you could stay inside and let others do the hard work for you. Some women actually resorted to having leeches drain their blood to achieve optimum paleness.

Loving yourself is important for transmutation because many humans who do not love the people they were have a more difficult time with transmutation. It is a little ironic that not being able to love your human body may cause you to be tied to it when your consciousness is ready to move on. Connecting to your higher self will help you understand why you chose this particular human form for this particular lifetime. Because beauty standards are constantly changing, you must learn to love yourself and accept your human body so that you may learn why you chose to have particular human characteristics that you do not like right now. Continue connecting with your higher self. Also, after I have placed the sacred geometric symbol in your heart chakra, you may wish to activate a different geometric symbol. If that is the case, conduct the earlier explained sequence again.

Loving who you are raises your frequency and assists the overall frequency of humanity. When your heart chakra illuminates your activated sacred geometric symbol, it will have a positive effect on other humans. This will likely happen on a subconscious level. Perhaps it will give someone else (on a subconscious level) the idea to read these pages. Or perhaps it will just give another human the desire to be kinder to himself or herself. Whatever the outcome, connecting with your higher self will give you a much greater perspective and insight into other humans.

Thank you for allowing me to connect with you. It has been my honor.

COMMENTARY BY ANUBIS

While every chapter in this book is important, Aphrodite's and Kwan Yen's chapters are ones that every human should read and review. Loving yourself is hard to do until you have forgiven yourself or someone else for a particular transgression. To do this, you must be able to connect with the energy of compassion, heal, and move on. Every human contains emotional scars. Some scars are from childhood, and some are from later in life. Being able to heal and forgive is not easy for humans. Most of the time, humans seem to ruminate on the negative parts of their lives. And sometimes, humans begin to enjoy the negative feelings that are attached to the negative parts of their lives because they are either used to feeling that way or they do not want to let go (because letting go would sometimes mean that they would have to begin living differently). For some reason, humans seem to be resistant to change (even positive change). Sometimes humans would rather focus on the negative things that have happened to them because this enables them to continue an addiction that they do not want to stop. Reliving past trauma allows this addiction to continue and grow. And humans have a difficult time stopping addictive behavior once they have started it. Humans who develop a love for their addiction(s) are difficult to change. Humans who are not able to stop an addiction before transmutation likely end up spending time with me in the underworld. The consciousness that has been active in this lifetime will need to understand why another human life will have to be lived for the purpose of being able to live free of addiction.

Also, I spend time with an infinite number of energies. There is a difference, however, between spending time with me because it is your choice and spending time with me because you must. Rehabilitation must take place within your human life or upon transmutation. If you are reading this book, however, you are ready to progress forward in your life.

CHAPTER 6

KWAN YEN

My name is a shortened form of a name that means one who sees and hears the cry from the human world. I am surnamed Sung-Tzu-Niang-Niang, which means lady who brings children. I am the goddess of fecundity as well as of mercy. I am worshiped especially by women. I comfort the troubled, sick, lost, senile, and unfortunate. I also care for souls in the underworld. I am invoked during post-burial rituals to free the soul of the deceased from the torments of purgatory.

As Aphrodite and Anubis have stated, this chapter should be read in conjunction with chapter five. While Aphrodite's energy assisted you with understanding how to love and forgive yourself, this chapter will be about how to love and forgive others. Humans seem to find it difficult to move on if they feel there are unfinished affairs on Earth. But the best way to transition is to forgive those before your transition. This may be the most difficult thing to do, and thus, it makes this one of the most important things to learn how to do before transitioning. Some of you will need to practice forgiveness every day. Letting go of those bindings will allow you to experience true peace and happiness.

Also like Aphrodite, my vibrational frequency is very high. So the frequency of this chapter will remain at the same frequency as the last chapter: 888 hertz.

Before starting, I want to say that this chapter may be difficult for many humans. This is because most humans find it difficult to let go of past transgressions. Holding onto those feelings assists humans in creating the walls that keep others out. But forgiving others is not for the sake of others; it is for the sake of oneself. Sometimes humans do not want to forgive because they get so used to feeling hatred or depression, especially when it comes to a particular person who has caused so much heartache. Many humans have been wronged by other humans. I am not saying that the transgressors' actions are OK. But the actions and being wronged and hurt teach humans very important lessons. This is one of them: letting go of that hatred, depression, etc. and transforming it into something new. Can you imagine loving that person or persons who have hurt you and caused you so much pain? We are all connected, and letting go of negative emotions helps raise the frequency of all humankind. This in turn assists with human evolution. Humans are not done evolving. Your race will be so different in the next few centuries. Some of you will be back, and some of you will be assisting those who are back as guides. You cannot, however, become a guide when you have not mastered the art of forgiveness. How can you guide another human into forgiveness when you are not able to get there yourself as a human? Working with me, you will.

As you work your way through these pages, you will feel lighter. Within each page and with each word that you read, you are working your way through forgiveness. Within each word, I have encoded energy, which will assist you to attain a higher frequency (if you wish). If you do not want this energy, you may block it by stating, "Kwan Yen, I do not wish to receive the frequency of forgiveness." Also, the encoding starts in the next paragraph, so those of you who do not wish to receive this transfer will not.

I would also like to address the number six. It symbolizes beauty and harmony. It is often called the love number. It holds the vibration of unconditional love, protection, and sanctuary. It holds the spiritual expression of the archetypal, maternal instincts that we all contain (whether male or female) and the primal urge to nurture and care for those in need. The number six represents service, both divine and human. In Latin script, the digit six has no sharp edges, and it even appears to resemble the pregnant female form.

The number six pertains to creation and completeness. The Pythagoreans believed six to be the first perfect number. A perfect number is one where the sum of all its divisors—excluding the number itself—equals the number itself, so 1 + 2 + 3 = 6. Perfect numbers are rare. The ancient Greeks recognized only four perfect numbers: 6, 28, 496, and 8,128. Snowflakes are droplets of water that have frozen into a hexagonal form. Six molecules of water are at the core of each one. Six is the atomic number for carbon, the element that is the basis for all life here on Earth.

Quartz crystal is made up of silicon atoms arranged in hexagonal patterns. Bees build their honeycombs hexagonally. Tortoiseshells, fish scales, and the skin of reptiles are all based on the same hexagonal form. If you cut into a carrot or across the top of a tomato, you'll see the hex forming its structure. Even human cells tessellate closely using this pattern of sixes.

People who have picked this number likely have personalities that are fair-minded, justice-driven, trusting, and honest. The six is also highly creative (containing double the essence of the three), caring, protective, and selfless. But its energy is also highly efficient. This can be seen in nature in the wax comb made by honeybees. This hexagonal shape with three-corner joints creates the greatest interior space in each interior cell with the least labor and materials.

Bees and Their Hive

Efficiency is a priority for those who choose the six. People with an abundance of this number put the needs of others ahead of their own to their detriment. Understanding how to put up proper boundaries tends to be an important lesson.

Sixes are deeply creative and strive to make things better. On the shadow side, sixes can become too controlling, forcing others to live up to unrealistic expectations. When a person with a strong sense of the number six is under stress, his or her maternal instinct can become intrusive and interfering, and its vibrational pattern may tend toward a self-righteous attitude. But it usually takes a major betrayal to bring that side of the six's nature to the foreground.

To start the process of forgiveness, we are going to talk about the kundalini. (I am going to assist in its awakening.) In Hinduism, kundalini (or coiled snake) is a form of divine feminine energy (or Shakti) located at the base of the spine in the root chakra.

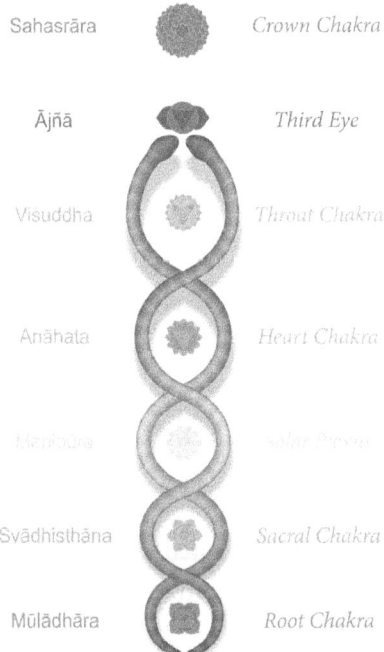

Chakras and Kundalini

It is a force or power associated with the divine feminine or the formless aspect of the Goddess. This energy in the body when cultivated and awakened is believed to lead to spiritual liberation.

Most humans have energetic blocks and imbalances as well as energy-sabotaging habits, which prevent you from accessing your full vitality. This leads to feeling exhausted, scattered, and even ill. Kundalini awakening offers an opportunity for you to expand your consciousness and begin to understand how expansive the universe is. It helps you to separate from your ego and release unhealthy patterns and habits. Old negative thoughts and pain begin to dissolve as the awakening energy begins to clean your old paradigm.

It is important to address why the kundalini is depicted as a snake. For some reason, many humans deem snakes as being negative. I don't understand why this is so. Despite its spiritual significance, the snake or the serpent is associated with so many negative connotations. These include evil, lies, and temptation. But snakes possess powerful spiritual energies. Signifying life force, the snake is a spirit animal in several cultures. It is viewed as a symbol of power, fertility, rebirth, and healing. The snake has been associated with healing for centuries. It has been used as the symbol of healing powers. Asclepius, the Greek god of medicine, was shown as two snakes climbing up a rod. This symbol, known as caduceus, is used all over the world as the symbol of medicine and healing. It makes sense that the snake would symbolize the kundalini; it is a symbol of spiritual healing. It also stands for spiritual liberation. Snakes represent transition, rebirth, and a fresh start. Because the snake sheds its skin, it signifies periods of transition. Snake energy encourages you to open your eyes and be who you truly are. It encourages you to live your own life. You don't need to do certain things to please people. Rather, do things based on what's right.

Right before this energy is activated, people usually dream of serpents or goddesses, which are the signs of this energy becoming activated. The transcriptionist had a dream in which she was holding a sword. At the base of this sword was a snake. At times, the snake would uncoil around the sword and then recoil at the base. This is the type of symbolism to be aware of in your dreams or meditations.

To be able to integrate this spiritual energy, a period of careful purification and strengthening of the body and nervous system is usually required. This is because the energy from the awakening of the kundalini is strong, and it takes some time to integrate through the human body. The transcriptionist studied for years before being able to integrate this energy throughout her body.

You must also note that there are physical manifestations of your kundalini awakening and uncoiling. Many kundalini-awakening symptoms result from changes to the nervous system. Symptoms are a sign of healing and of your body trying to maintain homeostasis or to increase your energy.

While kundalini awakening can be overwhelming and terrifying, it's also very primal and incredibly powerful. As the energy moves up your spine like a coiled snake, the experience can be very blissful, or it can be very frightening and intense. One thing you can be sure of is that when the kundalini is awakened, the life you know will never be the same again. This knowledge and understanding can be disturbing to some, so it is important to be very honest with yourself and to ask yourself whether you are ready for this type of understanding to enter your life. For certain individuals, the experience is slow and steady; for others, it's intense and immediate. The important thing is not to obsess over the symptoms but to find ways to allow the energy to move, healing the body and opening up the channels of energy. The awakening of the kundalini has numerous benefits.

- Better digestion and sleep.
- Enhanced motor skills, memory recall, and concentration.
- Hemispheric synchronization. (The left and right hemispheres of your brain will begin to operate at the same frequency.)
- Heightened awareness, spontaneous trance states, and mystical experiences.
- Deep peace, serenity, and a profound knowing of wisdom.

- Becoming conscious and connected with internal energies, intuition, and inner truth.
- Reviewing and recalling past-life experiences.
- Seeing the world move in a connected way.
- Discovering your soul's purpose and connecting with your destiny.

There are many more; these are just some of the benefits. Also, not all of these happen right away. The energy transfer I am going to give you will allow you to briefly experience this energy. You will need to continue on a spiritual path if you want to uncoil your kundalini. The insight I am going to give you will assist with your ability to forgive those whom you have not yet been able to forgive.

For this energy transfer, you must make sure that you have not had any alcohol within the last twenty-four hours. And you should not have ingested any mind-altering substances for the same amount of time. Because of the strength of this energy transfer, you should be clearheaded. (Being altered from meditation, however, is completely fine.) You should either be lying down or sitting up with your feet on the floor. If you are lying down, neither your arms nor legs should be crossed. Focus on your spine—particularly the base of your spine. Picture energy swirling around the base of your spine. You should be conscious of your breathing. Inhale for three counts, hold it for three, and then exhale for three counts. Hold an image of me in your mind's eye and think of my energy wrapping you like a blanket. You should feel comforted and at peace. Next, focus on my energy. It will be gathering at your crown chakra. When you are ready for me to activate your kundalini, give my energy permission to enter through your crown chakra and travel to the root of your spine. Permission may be given as a feeling or a thought. There are no specific words that you need to say.

Give my energy a few minutes to pass down your spine. You may feel a cooling sensation throughout your body. My energy will collect at the base of your spine and at the location of your kundalini. But take time to allow your body to get used to my energy. Some of you will not need this extra time, but some of you will. It is OK if you want to discontinue this exercise and begin again at another time. Just know that at every step, you are safe. Because awakening your kundalini may be startling for some of you (as I indicated earlier), feeling some discomfort may occur. This is because you might not be ready to receive or understand some of the spiritual messages, which can be significantly different from how you are used to thinking. I understand that realizing you have lived through several lifetimes can be jarring. Because the next thought for some of you will be, *What happened to those forms of consciousness once I passed on?* Were you exactly the same as you are now, or were those forms of consciousness significantly different? Again, these thoughts are OK to have, but to move on and achieve a more enlightened form of consciousness in this lifetime are what we are trying to assist you with.

So once you are comfortable with my energy, and you have focused it around the base of your spine, it should continue to swirl in a clockwise motion. Allow it to envelope your kundalini. You may continue to experience coolness throughout your body. This may take another few minutes. But you will know once I have activated your kundalini. You may feel an electric charge or a tingling at the base of your spine. If you do not feel anything, that is OK. It seems that some of your activations will have to be subtle because too much of an activation may give you too much of an energetic push at this time. You may do this exercise once a month until you feel like your kundalini has been activated.

Before the next exercise, I recommend that you wait twenty-four hours to allow yourself to become used to this new energy. In the next exercise, I am going to explain how to use this energy to help with the act of forgiveness. Transmuting hatred, anger, frustration, etc. into peace, love, and calming energy is important for two reasons. First, when you pass on, it helps you leave your human body without feeling like you have unfinished business. Second, it helps you begin transmuting energy. So when your consciousness transmutes, you will have some experience with understanding how that process works.

The forgiveness exercise has two components. The first component entails you to think about one transgression that causes you to feel emotions that are considered negative. To help with this exercise, I have asked the transcriptionist to copy and paste something that is called The Emotion Wheel. The Emotion Wheel was created by Robert Plutchik to help people identify and describe the eight core emotions: joy, sadness, fear, anger, anticipation, surprise, disgust, and trust. It was part of his overarching psycho-evolutionary theory of emotion.

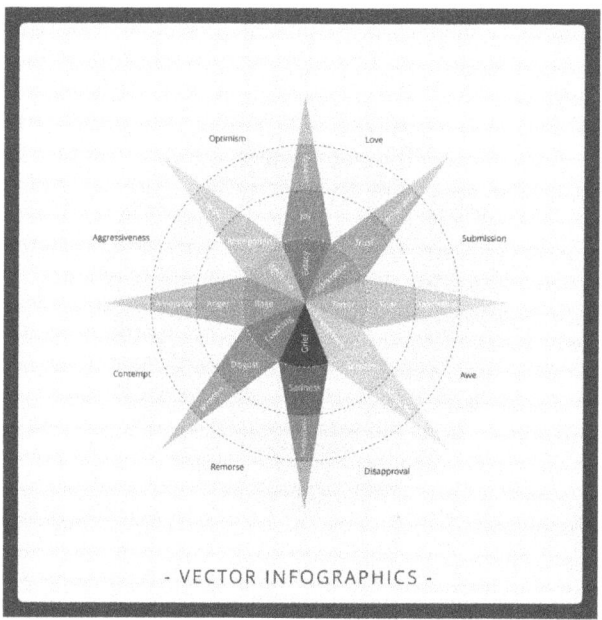

Emotion Wheel

His theory of emotion expanded on previous theories, some of which had labeled six primary emotions that all human beings feel. Plutchik believed that humans experience eight primary emotions. Each of these emotions has a polar opposite, which is also included on the wheel.

- Joy and its opposing emotion, sadness.
- Fear and its opposing emotion, anger.
- Anticipation and its opposing emotion, surprise.
- Disgust and its opposing emotion, trust.

You have probably found yourself in between two emotions. You feel joy, but you also feel anticipation. Maybe you're waiting for a check in the mail, or you are particularly excited about the year to come. Plutchik covered these emotions too. In between each emotion is an emotion that combines two adjoining emotions.

- Anticipation and joy: optimism.
- Anger and anticipation: aggressiveness.
- Joy and trust: love.
- Trust and fear: submission.
- Fear and surprise: awe.
- Surprise and sadness: disapproval.
- Sadness and disgust: remorse.
- Disgust and anger: contempt.

Sometimes, you might identify as just being happy, content, sad, or excited. Other times, your emotions may be complicated. Being nervous could be a good nervous or a bad nervous.

Identifying emotions is not an easy process, but it is crucial to being able to prepare for an easy process of consciousness transmutation. Take a moment to sit in a silent place and observe your body and mind. Do you feel tension anywhere in your body? Are your thoughts positive, negative, hopeful, etc.? Be patient and honest with yourself. Take five to ten minutes to go through this process.

Identifying your specific emotions builds emotional intelligence, which is important for transmutation. Emotional intelligence is the ability to identify and use emotions effectively. Emotional intelligence assists with

- Managing emotions before they turn into impulse behavior.
- Picking up on emotional cues and responding appropriately.
- Clearly communicating your goals and emotions to your partner, colleagues, or friends.
- Adapting to changing situations with ease.

- Remaining calm, even in scary or tense situations.
- Identifying strengths and weaknesses.
- Connecting thought patterns and physical responses with certain emotions.
- Knowing what events or topics may trigger strong emotions and preparing appropriately.

Let's go back to the forgiveness exercise. Think about the person who caused you to feel negative emotions and the act that this person did to make you feel negatively. As you think about this act and the emotions that it generates, picture those emotions rising above your head in a bubble. Really think about how you felt as you lived through this interaction. Think about how you felt as it was happening and then how you felt afterward. All the while, these emotions are rising above you, and they are being collected within a bubble. Take as much time as you need to generate all the emotions that you experienced. Once you feel that you have collected these emotions, ask me to come and collect the bubble that has formed above your head. When I collect these emotions, you will likely feel lighter.

Next, picture the person who caused these feelings, standing across from you. Picture me standing behind you. Now, place your hand (right or left) over the other person's heart and tell that the person following: "I take back my power." Feel every part of yourself come back from that other person. Once you feel that you have taken your power back, tell that person the following: "You no longer control my thoughts or feelings. I am done with you. You may go." You may continue to watch or not watch that person. If the act that caused a generation of negative feelings for you was done by more than one person, go through the exercise above with each person standing in front of you.

In all likelihood, several people have harmed you. While some of these transgressions were planned before coming into the body you currently inhabit (the purpose being for you to experience particular hardships), there is always a time when you must let this go. Going through this exercise does not mean that you will never think about this transgression and generate the same negative emotions again. That is OK. It just means that you have not yet fully forgiven the person (or persons) who harmed you. It means that you just need more time to forgive and let go. And when you are ready to let go, just go through this exercise again. Calling on me is very easy. All you need to do is follow the steps above as I have given them.

Forgiveness increases your emotional intelligence and assists with uncoiling the kundalini. I understand that many humans find it incredibly difficult to forgive. Many find it even more difficult to forget. I have often heard humans say, "I forgive you, but I will not forget what you did." Then what is the purpose of forgiveness? For you to move on, you must do both. Otherwise, you will not be able to break down the walls that you have formed because of the harmful event. I am not saying, however, to forget the lessons that you learned from that traumatic event—whether it is watching for certain red flags that a person may exhibit, keeping pepper spray or mace on your person when you are alone, etc.—I'm just saying that forgetting and forgiving go hand in hand.

This forgiveness exercise is also useful for forgiving certain physical aspects of your body. For example, someone who has chronic stomach issues might say things like, "Oh, I can't go out tonight because of my stupid stomach." Or perhaps you had surgery on a particular limb (like your leg), and that limb aches badly on a chronic basis. So you might say something like, "I move slowly because of my dumb leg." Consistently calling these parts of you stupid, dumb, etc. continually generates negative feelings and emotions about that particular limb or organ. And that organ or limb, while a part of you, also exists on its own. Think of it like your chakras. Sometimes those chakras close due to certain thoughts and practices that you did. And you must then take additional steps to reopen them and keep them moving in a clockwise direction. Every part of you exists in tandem with you, but it also exists independently. So that organ or limb knows that you have those negative feelings toward it.

So if you are experiencing chronic pain, I recommend connecting with that part of your body and forgiving it while also asking it to forgive you. This forgiveness exercise will be a little different than the one described above. The first step will be to connect with that part of yourself. Let's say you have chronic pain in your stomach. Place your hands on your stomach and try to connect with the energy emanating from it. Ask me to assist with connecting. Now, think of all the negative emotions that are connected with that part of yourself. Ask me to collect and remove them. Now, ask that part for forgiveness while stating that your forgiveness is also granted. I recommend also expressing your gratitude to that limb or organ for its hard work in continuing to assist you even while it is not able to work at its full capacity. Like forgiving a person, forgiving a part of yourself might take a few tries, especially if you have years of frustration and anger.

As you near the end of my chapter, I just want to explain why forgiveness is so important to your human experience. Forgiving gets you out of victim mode. Forgiveness breaks the bonds that tie you negatively to another person. What happened to you happened. There's no denying that. But when you are no longer a victim or controlled by negative energy, you can focus on becoming stronger, establishing your own integrity, and building your own character so that you know yourself well enough to never be caught in a situation of terrible compromise and pain again. Forgiveness also frees you. It allows you to take your power back. The energy and emotion you have so deeply invested in a certain person or situation are now free to be moved to someone or something that is positive for your growth and emotional, psychological, and physical health. You are no longer chained to an entity that saps your energy and takes the life out of you. And freeing yourself may allow you to see this person or situation in a whole different light. Instead of focusing on all the negatives, forgiving may allow you to remember all the positives that once were and still are there.

Forgiving helps you move forward on your spiritual path. It encourages compassion. You are able to relate to others as part of the human experience. You feel for others as you do for yourself. Emotionally and psychologically unencumbered, you can begin to put the past behind you. Forgiveness is an act of kindness and goodness. It is a path to peace.

Thank you for allowing me to share your life. As other energies have stated, it is difficult to reach many humans these days, particularly in the western world. Now that you are familiar with us and know how to contact us, you are able to learn more about us (if you wish to). I encourage you to do so. Our talents go beyond those that have been described in these short pages. (Well, it is short to us.) Each of us knows that it is difficult to be human. Compared to many other beings, Earthlings are very young. Those of you who are able to connect with other energies make it possible for other humans to continue to advance and evolve. Reading this book and engaging the energies within it are steps in that direction. Again, thank you for your time. I look forward to knowing you.

COMMENTARY BY ANUBIS

The end of this chapter marks a dynamic and energetic shift within these pages. The next few chapters are mostly written by male energies (except for The Witch and Hekate). I am looking forward to working with them and for you to work with them. Not as many people are familiar with Mimir as with the energies in the past few chapters. But Mimir is one of the most knowledgeable energies in existence. I know I make this statement before almost every chapter, but I am still going to state the obvious: I recommend that everyone reading this guide read the next chapter. Mimir is going to give you the ability to sift through other people's thoughts and energies so that they do not cloud your life's mission or purpose. Mimir is also going to give you more insight into the transmutation experience. While I will give you insight into the underworld (my realm), Mimir will give you some information as to why it is so important to prepare for the transmutation of your consciousness. There are certainly places that you do not want to go. And Mimir knows about and will explain what some of those places are. Indeed, sometimes you must know about the negative to appreciate the positive. And while humans do so much preparation for so many things in life, why is it that they believe the only preparation for transmutation is to plan a funeral? By that time, consciousness has left. They prepare for and plan birthdays, weddings, anniversaries, retirements, etc. The most important thing to plan and prepare for is the transmutation of the consciousness. I do hope that with the paradigm shift that is happening on Earth, humans understand how important it is to connect with their consciousness (or your higher selves) and prepare for that transition early on in life. These are just some of the reasons as to why I am so elated about this book. And with that, I will wish you happiness and love as you move on to Mimir's chapter.

CHAPTER 7

MIMIR

Greetings! I am so very pleased to be working with you. Because of entertainment media and marketing, many of you think of Thor or Odin as the Nordic gods. There are many more. And as my description explained in the beginning of this book, I am the one who asked for Odin's eye. He got something in exchange for it though. So that brings us to what I will need from you before you work with me. I have asked the transcriptionist for nothing in exchange for my participation in this book. I knew the transcriptionist in a former life, and she owes me nothing. If you choose to work with me, I ask for something very simple: Light a candle for me. Write my name on the candle and light it as many times as it takes until the wick no longer lights (or the candle is gone). Every time you light the candle, just say my name out loud three times. I know, three really is a magic number when it comes to divination and spiritual work.

Although the introduction gave a brief explanation of who I am, I would like to give a little more information. In Norse mythology, I am a god who is known for my wisdom and knowledge. I am said to be the wisest of all the gods. I am thus known for my ability to solve complex problems and provide counsel to other gods and humans.

I was beheaded during the Aesir-Vanir war.[9] Odin, the king of the gods, asked that I be resurrected. I agreed on the condition that I could return only as a head, which Odin placed in a well near his throne so that I could continue advising him. My wisdom and counsel are highly valued, and my name is often still associated with wisdom and knowledge.

Now, many of the other chapters have been of a more noncorporeal nature. Mine will be much more factual and will take you through some techniques that will lead you to living better while on this plane, which will then make your transition easier.

But first things first. If you chose the number seven, you are likely a person who is calm, wise, and deeply intuitive. In numerology, the number seven holds the vibration of the intellect, ideas, and higher wisdom. It often stands as a symbol for truth and perfection, as it's comprised of the numbers three (the number of Heaven (or Spirit) and four (the number of the Earth)).

The number seven can be described as the holiest and most magical of the cardinal numbers. The seven holds an intriguing set of qualities within its energetic weight—it is one of logical analysis and attaining understanding, but it also one of spirituality and mysticism. This analytical energy of number seven is full of vibrations, including heightened awareness, knowledge, understanding, logic, organization, and judgment.

The number seven is often associated with a range of energies and meanings in many cultures and spiritual traditions. From ancient times, seven has been seen as a sacred number, which holds great power and significance. One of the most common interpretations of the number seven is its association with the seven days of the week. In many cultures, each day is associated with a particular deity or force of nature. It is thought to carry its own energy and influence. For example, Sunday is often associated with the sun, and it is seen as a day of renewal and recharging while Friday is associated with love, and it is seen as a day to focus on relationships.

---

[9] The Aesir-Vanir war was a legendary conflict in Norse mythology between the Aesir, the gods of war and power, and the Vanir, the gods of fertility and prosperity. The war is said to have taken place at the beginning of time, and before the creation of the world as humans now know it. The conflict was eventually resolved through a peace treaty, in which the two groups of gods exchanged hostages to ensure that peace was maintained.

Another interpretation of the number seven is its association with the seven chakras, which are energy centers in the human body. In Hindu and yogic traditions, the chakras are thought to regulate the flow of energy through the body. They are associated with different aspects of our physical, emotional, and spiritual well-being. The number seven is seen as a powerful symbol of balance and harmony, as each chakra is thought to influence the others in a harmonious manner.

In numerology, seven is often seen as the number of spiritual growth and development. It is associated with introspection, meditation, and the pursuit of knowledge and wisdom. People who pick seven as their life-path number and in this guide are thought to be introspective and intuitive. They have a deep connection to the spiritual realm.

In astrology, seven is associated with the planet Neptune, which is often associated with dreams, intuition, and spirituality. People born under the sign of Pisces, which is ruled by Neptune, are often seen as sensitive and intuitive. They have a strong connection to the spiritual realm.

Finally, the number seven is often associated with the idea of completion and perfection. In many cultures, seven is seen as a number of completion and the end of a cycle. For example, the seven days of the week are seen as a complete cycle, and the seven stages of life are seen as a journey to completion.

The number seven holds a range of energies and meanings in different spiritual and cultural traditions. Whether associated with the days of the week, the chakras, numerology, astrology, or the idea of completion and perfection, seven is often seen as a powerful and sacred number, which holds great significance and influence.

In the tarot deck, the seven is represented by the Chariot. The Chariot is often seen as a symbol of strength, determination, and triumph. This card is associated with the astrological sign of Cancer, and it is typically depicted as a figure driving a chariot pulled by two horses, one black and one white. The chariot is often interpreted as a symbol of the journey of life. The figure driving the chariot is a representation of the individual's will and determination.

The Chariot card is often seen as a symbol of progress and movement. The chariot represents the journey of life, and the figure driving the chariot is interpreted as being in control of his or her own destiny. This card is often seen as a reminder that we have the power to shape our own lives and to make progress toward our goals.

The two horses that pull the chariot, one black and one white, represent the opposing forces in our lives, such as light and darkness, good and evil, or order and chaos. The figure driving the chariot is able to harness these opposing forces and use them to move forward, demonstrating mastery over his or her own inner struggles and ability to overcome obstacles.

In many tarot decks, the Chariot card is also associated with the qualities of strength and determination. The figure driving the chariot is often depicted wearing armor and holding a shield, suggesting that he or she is prepared for battle and is ready to face any challenges that come his or her way. This card is often interpreted as a reminder that we need to be strong and determined in pursuit of our goals and to maintain our focus and resolve, even in the face of adversity.

Another aspect of the Chariot card is its association with the idea of victory. The chariot is often depicted as a symbol of triumph. The figure driving the chariot is seen as a conqueror. This card is often interpreted as a reminder that we have the power to overcome obstacles and to achieve our goals and that victory is within our reach if we remain determined and focused.

As with any association with the number seven, the Chariot card in the tarot is a powerful symbol of strength, determination, and triumph. It represents the journey of life and the power of the individual to shape his or her own destiny.

In this chapter, you will be using the quantum field. The quantum field is a concept in physics that describes the underlying reality of the universe. It is based on the idea that everything in the universe is made up of tiny particles, which are constantly interacting with each other. These particles are not only physical objects but also forces like gravity and electromagnetism.

The quantum field is different from the classical field that we experience in our everyday lives. For example, in a classical field, a particle exists in a specific place at a specific time. In a quantum field, however, particles are not so well defined. Instead, they exist as probabilities, and they can be in multiple places at once.

One way to think of the quantum field is to imagine it as a vast network of interactions between particles. Every time a particle interacts with another particle, it creates a ripple in the quantum field, which spreads out and influences other particles. This creates a kind of dance between particles, where they are constantly interacting and influencing one another.

The idea of the quantum field is closely tied to the concept of quantum mechanics, which is a theory that explains how particles behave at the subatomic level.[10] Quantum mechanics has been extremely successful in explaining many phenomena that cannot be explained by

---

[10] Quantum mechanics is a branch of physics that deals with the behavior of matter and energy at the subatomic level. It is based on the idea that particles, like electrons and photons, can exist in multiple states at the same time. They can be in different places simultaneously. This is in contrast to classical mechanics, which assumes that particles exist in specific places and have specific properties at all times.

One of the key ideas in quantum mechanics is that particles do not have a definite location or trajectory. Instead, they exist as probabilities. Their behavior can be predicted only in terms of the probability of finding them in a particular place or with a particular velocity. This is a very different way of thinking about the world compared to classical physics, in which particles have a definite location and trajectory.

Another important idea in quantum mechanics is the concept of wave-particle duality. This means that particles can display both wavelike and particle-like behavior, depending on how they are being observed. For example, when a particle passes through a narrow slit, it can produce a wave pattern on a screen, but when it is detected, it behaves like a particle. This duality is a central feature of quantum mechanics. It is still not fully understood.

Quantum mechanics also includes the idea of superposition, which means that particles can exist in multiple states at the same time. This is known as the principle of indeterminacy. It means that the state of a particle cannot be precisely determined until it is observed.

One of the most famous and strange concepts in quantum mechanics is the idea of entanglement. This is the idea that particles can become connected in such a way that their properties become correlated, even when separated by great distances. This has been experimentally verified, and it is considered one of the central ideas of quantum mechanics.

classical physics. For example, it has been used to explain why particles can be in multiple places at once, why particles can become entangled and share properties across great distances, and why particles can change their behavior depending on how they are being observed.

The quantum field is also related to the concept of entanglement, which is the idea that particles can be connected to each other in such a way that their properties become correlated, even when separated by great distances. This is a strange and counterintuitive idea, but it has been experimentally verified. It is considered one of the central ideas of quantum mechanics.

The quantum field is a concept in physics that describes the underlying reality of the universe. It is based on the idea that everything in the universe is made up of particles, which are constantly interacting with each other. These interactions create a vast network of influences, which shape the behavior of particles. The quantum field is closely tied to the concepts of quantum mechanics and entanglement, and it has been extremely successful in explaining many phenomena that cannot be explained by classical physics. While the idea of the quantum field may seem strange and counterintuitive, it is a fundamental concept in our understanding of the universe and the nature of reality.

The quantum field can be thought of as a vast ocean of energy and information. Just as an ocean has countless individual droplets of water that make up the whole, the quantum field is made up of countless individual particles that are constantly interacting and influencing one another.

Each particle in the quantum field is like a tiny ripple in the ocean. Every time a particle interacts with another particle, it creates a new ripple, which spreads out and influences other particles. These ripples create a complex network of interactions, which shape the behavior of particles, just as waves in the ocean interact and create patterns of movement.

Just as an ocean can appear calm on the surface but contain hidden currents and tides below, the quantum field can appear stable and unchanging, but in reality, it is constantly in flux. Its particles interact and influence one another.

And just as the ocean can appear differently depending on the perspective of the observer, the quantum field can also display different properties depending on how it is being observed. This is related to the concept of wave-particle duality, where particles can display both wavelike and particle-like behavior.

Do you understand why I am known as the god of wisdom? Let's take this one step further. Through me, you are going to learn how to use the quantum field of consciousness, which is part of the quantum field. The concept of a quantum field of consciousness explains that consciousness, like subatomic particles, is a field of energy and information, which permeates the universe and connects all things. To use the quantum field of consciousness, it's important to have a clear and focused intention. We are going to use the quantum field of consciousness to learn how to live with energies that negatively influence us instead of fighting them.

What do I mean when I say negative energies? There are many different ways that negative energies manifest and affect individuals and communities. Here are a few examples.

1. Fear

Fear is a powerful negative energy, which can cause anxiety, stress, and paranoia. It can arise from perceived or real threats and can create a sense of unease and instability.

2. Anger

Anger is an intense negative energy, which can arise from feelings of frustration, injustice, or disappointment. When left unchecked, anger can lead to conflict and violence.

3. Hatred

Hatred is a strong and intense form of anger, which is directed toward a specific person or group. It is a destructive energy, which can lead to prejudice, discrimination, and violence.

4. Jealousy

Jealousy is a negative energy, which arises from feelings of insecurity and inadequacy. It can lead to feelings of resentment and bitterness, undermine relationships, and cause conflict.

5. Guilt

Guilt is a negative energy, which arises from feelings of remorse or regret. It can be a powerful and persistent energy, which can lead to feelings of shame and self-doubt.

6. Grief

Grief is a negative energy, which arises from the loss of someone or something important to us. It can cause feelings of sadness, depression, and helplessness.

7. Envy

Envy is a negative energy, which arises from a desire for what others have. It can lead to feelings of resentment and dissatisfaction, undermine relationships, and cause conflict.

These are just a few examples of the many different negative feelings and thoughts that can negatively affect your life and interrupt your ability to focus on living to learn your ultimate lesson. Someone else's negativity can affect you in several ways, depending on the intensity and duration of the negativity, as well as your level of awareness and resilience. Here are a few ways that someone else's negativity can impact you.

1. Emotional Contagion

Emotions can be contagious. When you are around someone who is expressing negative emotions such as anger, frustration, or sadness, you may start to feel those same emotions. This can be particularly true if you are empathetic or sensitive to the emotions of others.

2. Energy Drain

Negative people can be energy vampires, draining your energy and leaving you feeling depleted or exhausted. This can be particularly true if you are in a close relationship or work environment with someone who is consistently negative.

3. Stress and Anxiety

Negative people can create a stressful or anxious environment, particularly if their negativity is directed toward you. This can lead to physical and emotional symptoms, such as an increased heart rate, muscle tension, and difficulty concentrating.

4. Reduced Self-Esteem

If you are consistently around someone who is negative, you may start to internalize that person's messages and beliefs. This leads to reduced self-esteem and confidence.

Overall, someone else's negativity can have a significant impact on your well-being, particularly if it is persistent and intense. It is important to recognize the signs of negative influence and to take steps to protect yourself, such as setting boundaries, practicing self-care, and seeking support from others.

Moreover, it may be difficult to rid yourself of negative feelings that are either created by you or by someone else because of your ego. The ego—from a spiritual perspective—is seen as a limiting factor, which creates a sense of separation and division and prevents individuals from realizing their true natures and connection to the universe. Many spiritual traditions view the ego as an illusion, which must be transcended in order to achieve a state of unity and connection with the divine.

The ego is often described as the little self. It represents our limited sense of who we are and what we want in life. It is driven by our desires, fears, and insecurities. It creates a sense of duality, distinguishing the self from the rest of the world. This duality can lead to feelings of loneliness, anxiety, and stress, as well as a constant need to prove ourselves to others.

From a spiritual perspective, the ego can be seen as a hindrance to growth and spiritual development. It blocks our ability to experience the world in a pure and unencumbered way. It creates a sense of separation from others and the divine. This separation can lead to feelings of loneliness and disconnection and can prevent one from experiencing the deeper truth and purpose of life.

I am going to teach you how to use the quantum field of consciousness to remove your ego for a little while. You should note that humans need their egos for survival—it assists with fight or flight—so it should never be permanently removed. It's what makes you human. The technique I will teach you will remove your ego for thirty minutes. There are ways to increase that time span. But for beginners, thirty minutes will be the amount of time that this will occur.

Let's start by looking at a unicursal hexagram. A unicursal hexagram is a six-pointed star or hexagram, which can be traced or drawn in one continuous line without lifting a pen or pencil. Unlike a regular hexagram, which is formed by two triangles overlapping, a unicursal hexagram has a single path that connects all six points in a continuous loop.

Unicursal Hexagram

There are a few interesting things about the unicursal hexagram.

1. It is a symbol of unity and wholeness. The unicursal hexagram is a unique and powerful symbol, which represents the integration and balance of opposing forces, such as the masculine and feminine, the conscious and unconscious, and the spiritual and material. It is often used as a talisman or amulet to promote harmony and balance in one's life.

2. It has mystical and occult associations. The unicursal hexagram is a popular symbol in various esoteric and mystical traditions, such as Thelema, Wicca, and Hermeticism. It is often used in rituals, spells, and meditations to invoke spiritual energies and connect with the divine.

3. It has connections to the Tarot. The unicursal hexagram is associated with the Tarot card "The Lovers in the Thoth Tarot deck, which is often interpreted as representing the union of opposites and the integration of the conscious and unconscious.

4. It is a challenging design to create. Unlike a regular hexagram, which can be easily drawn by overlapping two triangles, the unicursal hexagram requires a continuous line, which connects all six points without lifting the pen or pencil. This makes it a challenging design to create and gives it a sense of uniqueness and mystique.

Overall, the unicursal hexagram is a fascinating and powerful symbol, which has many different meanings and associations in various spiritual and mystical traditions. Its unique design and deep symbolism make it a popular choice for those seeking to connect with their spirituality and tap into the mysteries of the universe.

As a tie-in to Aphrodite's chapter, a unicursal hexagram is considered to be a form of sacred geometry. Again, sacred geometry refers to the belief that certain geometric shapes and patterns have inherent spiritual or mystical significance, that they can be used to connect with the divine, and that they can promote spiritual growth and healing. The unicursal hexagram is considered sacred for the reasons given above.

While you look into the unicursal hexagram, you must give me permission to remove your ego. I will not remove your ego without your permission. So if you wish, you may continue to read through this chapter without actively going through these steps. Everyone should proceed at his or her own pace.

After giving me permission to remove your ego, close your eyes. When you close your eyes, you should still be able to see the unicursal hexagram. While you focus on the unicursal hexagram with your eyes closed, place your hands over your heart and ask the unicursal hexagram to take you to the quantum field. The first time you ask, feel your vibrational frequency and visualize it 10 percent above where you are. Take a deep breath. With your hands still over your heart, ask the unicursal hexagram a second time to take you to the quantum field. When you ask a second time, feel your vibrational frequency and visualize it 20 percent above where you are. Take another deep, cleansing breath. With your hands still over your heart, ask the unicursal hexagram a third time to take you to the quantum field. Now, feel your vibrational frequency and visualize it 30 percent above where you are. You may continue to do this until you can feel your consciousness drifting in the quantum field.

If you feel like you are having difficulty raising your awareness into the quantum field, you may ask me for assistance. When you focus on the quantum field, you may start to experience a sense of unity and interconnectedness with all things, as you will become more attuned to the underlying patterns and vibrations of reality. You may also experience a sense of expanded awareness or heightened intuition, as you will be able to tap into the deeper levels of consciousness, which underlie everyday reality. You may also feel a sense of peace and tranquility, as you let go of the limitations and constraints of everyday life and connect with the infinite possibilities of the quantum realm.

If you are new to meditation or are raising your consciousness for the first time, you may need to try this more than once. Some of you may be focusing too much on an immediate feeling or supernatural experience. It does not work like that. You have to open yourself up to the possibility if you want the possibility to come to you. Letting go of the human need to see or feel something tangible is difficult to do. But when you work at it, the ultimate result is exceedingly rewarding.

Once your consciousness is in the quantum field, and once you feel relaxed, ask me to remove your ego. You will not feel anything negative from this removal technique. You may, however, feel lighter and less restricted by fear or anxiety. While in this state, you will understand why the negative energies, which I explained earlier, should really have no place in your life. Why does it matter whether someone else spoke negatively about you or not? Perhaps those words were motivated by jealousy, fear, etc. The majority of the time, the motivating factor behind unkind words or feelings is a person's ego. And the majority of the time when you are impacted by those unkind words or feelings, the worry, stress, or anxiety that is caused by those unkind words comes from your ego.

When you are in the quantum field or while your ego is removed, you may begin to understand the concept that we are all interconnected.

All living beings, as well as the natural world and the universe as a whole, are expressions of the same underlying consciousness or energy. This means that every individual is a part of the larger whole and that there is no fundamental separation between any two things in the universe.

Once again, one way to understand this concept is through the metaphor of the ocean and its waves. Just as the waves are temporary expressions of the larger ocean, individual beings and things are seen as temporary expressions of the larger unified consciousness. In this way, every person, animal, plant, and even inanimate object is considered to be part of the same interconnected whole. The understanding that we are all one has important implications for the way you see yourself and for your relationship with the world and the people in it. It suggests that there is no other or enemy because we are all part of the same underlying consciousness. This belief can also inspire a sense of empathy and compassion for others.

Overall, the concept that we are all one suggests that there is a deep and fundamental connection between all living beings and the universe as a whole. Recognizing and embracing this connection can lead to greater spiritual, ethical, and moral understanding and growth.

By living with the knowledge that all consciousness is interconnected, you will be able to peacefully accept that when your consciousness transmutes from this planet, you will begin the steps to the next part of your journey again. I say again because, as it has been said in previous chapters, you have lived hundreds of thousands of lifetimes already. Some of you remember some past lives, and some of you do not. Sometimes humans don't remember much of a past life or lives because they aren't able to wrap their minds around how that works. And that's fine. But you do gain a deeper understanding of the universe when you are able to accept this as a fact.

Why are past lives difficult for some to accept? It may go against what some people have been taught. In Christianity, past lives are not discussed. It is thought that people have only one life. However, the belief in past lives is deeply rooted in several spiritual and religious traditions around the world. In Hinduism, Buddhism, and Jainism, reincarnation is a central tenet. These religions have been practiced for thousands of years. They have millions of followers who believe in the cycle of birth and rebirth. Similarly, the concept of reincarnation is also present in ancient Egyptian, Greek, and Celtic mythology. The fact that so many cultures and religions throughout history have embraced the idea of past lives suggests that it is more than just a fanciful notion.

Furthermore, many people report having vivid memories of events and experiences from a past life. These memories can often be triggered by visiting a certain place or meeting someone with whom they feel an instant connection. While some skeptics may dismiss these memories as mere imagination or fantasy, there are countless cases of people who have been able to provide details about their past lives, which could not have been obtained through any other means. Some individuals have even been able to speak in languages that they have never learned in their current life, indicating that these skills were acquired in a previous existence.

Many people have unexplained phobias or fears that cannot be traced back to any particular event in their current life. For example, a person may have a debilitating fear of water despite never having had a negative experience with it. It is possible that this fear is a manifestation of a traumatic experience in a past life. The idea of past lives is also supported by the concept of energy and the interconnectedness of all things. You are made up of energy, and this energy is constantly flowing and changing. As stated in the introduction to this book, when you die, your energy does not simply disappear; it is transformed and reused in other forms. This means the energy that once made up your physical body can be used to form a new one in a future life.

As my chapter is concluding, I would just like to encourage each of you to dig deeper. Dig deeper into your thoughts and the core of your being. Who would you like to be? How would you like to be remembered? Have you helped anyone in his or her journey, or have you been focused solely on yourself? Have you been concerned with making money (more than just the money needed to pay your bills)? Because you're reading this guide, you're on the right track to increasing your frequency and getting closer to the things you need to do to level up. Thank you for including me in your life practice (and now your death preparation).

COMMENTARY BY ANUBIS

Thank you, Mimir. This chapter added some different tools for those of you who perhaps needed to discuss transmutation logically. The next chapter, Hekate or The Witch, will be very different. There will be many references to rituals and pagan practices. I encourage those who connected with Mimir, however, to read this next chapter and maybe even try some of the practices. That is how you will expand your way of thinking and perhaps your life.

CHAPTER 8

HEKATE AND THE WITCH

Next to magick, death or transmutation is our favorite topic. We will be incorporating magick into this chapter so that you may understand your power and control over your own transmutation. Living your life like it is magick (because it is) can become an important tool in making your transmutation seamless and exciting.

There are two reasons that you could have picked the number eight. You are either connected with the frequency of the number or are connected to The Witch. (You have lived a past life in which you were connected to her, or you are connected to her in your current life.)

Let's talk about the number eight. It is often associated with abundance, success, and achievement. It is considered to be a powerful and influential number, representing the manifestation of goals and desires. It is also associated with balance and harmony, as it is symmetrical, and it can be divided equally. It is often seen as a representation of karma, as the energy that is put out into the world is believed to come back in equal measure. Furthermore, the number eight is associated with financial and material success. This is because the shape of the number resembles the symbol for infinity, indicating the potential for infinite abundance and wealth. It is often seen as a symbol of power and authority, as those who possess the qualities of this number are believed to be strong, confident, and driven.

In the tarot, the number eight is associated with the Strength card. The Strength card is typically depicted as a woman taming a lion or a similar wild animal. It represents the idea of inner strength, courage, and the ability to overcome obstacles through willpower and determination.

The Strength card is often seen as a symbol of spiritual power and self-mastery. It suggests that humans have the ability to overcome their fears and limitations by tapping into their inner strengths and wisdom. The card is also associated with patience, perseverance, and the ability to stay focused on goals despite setbacks and challenges.

The Strength card is associated with the astrological sign of Leo, which is known for its confidence, leadership, and creative energy. The card is often seen as a symbol of the divine masculine energy, representing the courage, assertiveness, and action-oriented qualities that are associated with this archetype.

People who feel connected to the number eight are often ambitious, driven, and goal-oriented individuals. They are focused on achieving success and are willing to work hard to make their dreams a reality. People who resonate with the number eight are often confident, assertive, and self-assured. They are not afraid to take risks and are willing to do what it takes to succeed. They are often seen as natural leaders and are respected for their abilities to inspire and motivate others.

THE WITCH

As stated in the introduction to this book, I am a member of an ancient coven called the Komati. I say "am," because we are all together on the other side of the veil. We originated in Africa and then eventually settled in India. The Komati did not accept men. We were all women who had exceptional powers. Our coven had four wolves, all of whom traveled with us to India. I began transcribing what would eventually be called the *Book of the Dead*. After its transcription, each coven member of the Komati took a vow in blood to protect this book. While there are numerous chapters, I have agreed to allow this information on transmutation to be communicated. (Actually, all the members of the coven had to be in agreement for this information to be released at this particular time.) In the coven, every woman had a specific role. Each role was connected to a specific direction. My role in the coven was to act as its soul. I represented the southeastern direction. So I brought the elements of air and fire together.

The element of air represents the realm of the mind, thought, communication, and intellect. It is associated with the direction of east, the season of spring, and the time of dawn. It is also represented by the suit of swords in the tarot, which is often associated with intellect, communication, and conflict. The element of air is often linked to the qualities of clarity, intellect, and communication. It is associated with the power of the spoken and written word, as well as the ability to analyze and reason. Air is also associated with the realm of ideas and inspiration. It is often called upon to help access intuition and imagination. Air is also associated with breath, which is essential for life. Breathing exercises and meditations are often used in witchcraft to connect with the element of air and bring balance to the mind and body.

The element of fire represents transformation, passion, energy, creativity, and strength. Fire is associated with the direction of the south, the season of summer, and the time of noon. It is also represented by the suit of wands in the tarot, which is often associated with creativity, passion, and inspiration. The element of fire is often linked to the qualities of courage, willpower, and the ability to overcome obstacles. It is associated with the power of the will, the ability to take action, and the power of transformation and change. Fire is associated with the realm of passion and creativity. It is often called on to help access inspiration and energy. Fire is associated with the sun, which is essential for life and is a symbol of vitality and power. Sun rituals and meditations are used in witchcraft to connect with the element of fire and bring strength and vitality to the practitioner and her surroundings.

The Komati often invoked Hekate while performing rituals and blessings. We also invoked her when we transcribed the *Book of the Dead*. Although transmutation is the topic of this guide, it is my belief that if you can experience magick on this plane, you will come to understand how energy (and therefore transmutation) works. So this chapter is going to address how you can incorporate magick into your life and experience something that is perhaps outside what humans believe to be the realm of possibilities. Before beginning, however, I am going to give the floor to Hekate.

HEKATE

Blessed be. I am so excited to be working with you. As some of you know, I am able to walk in both worlds (the underworld and the world above). While the underworld is not what some religions make it out to be (fire and brimstone), there is such a place. When I walk the underworld, it is always for a specific purpose. Sometimes it is to retrieve a soul who is ready to cross from the underworld. Sometimes it is to connect to a certain energy. There are very few energies that are able to walk in both worlds, which is why I am one of the few energies who may be invoked when information is requested regarding the *Book of the Dead*.

I am excited to give you some easy spells and activities that you can do to begin incorporating magick into your life. Some of you may already know some of the information that we are going to give in this chapter. I am going to have this transcriptionist prepare a book in the future with more advanced spells, which will incorporate some things that were not around in previous spells. In that next book, I will give you tools to be able to invoke the directional elements and energies and how to bring down the moon during a ritual. But that will be later. So now let's begin with some information about magick. (At this point, the narration of this chapter will be both myself and The Witch.)

TYPES OF SPELLS

There are a few categories of spells. Here are the main ones:

- Banishing: To banish means to cast something or someone out of your life. If it's a person, the spell will stop that individual from seeing you or even thinking about you. Some practitioners use banishing spells to get rid of negative entities.
- Binding: To bind means to control or limit the target's power. The idea behind this type of ritual is to symbolically tie up someone or something so that you can restrict his or her actions and prevent that person from harming himself, herself, or others. While casting these spells on a person is not advisable, you can cast a binding spell on yourself, for example, to break a bad habit. The transcriptionist cast a binding spell on herself in a past life. She has it staying in place for every future life.
- Freezing: Similar to binding spells, a freezer spell is typically used when you want to silence someone—freezing someone's actions or words. The most common is to write down the name of the target and place the paper in the freezer.
- Sweetening: Commonly known as honey jars, sweetening spells try to sweeten or mellow someone's attitude toward you. A sweetening spell may be cast on a specific person or situation (such as a legal case, a career problem, or a relationship). A representation of the target is placed in a jar (a name, personal belonging, sigil, etc.), and honey is added on top.
- Protection: Feeling safe and protected is the most valuable gift as a sentient being. In ancient times, shamans and healers would help people to cure diseases, remove ailments, and feel stronger.
- Good Luck: To invite good luck is a way to empower ourselves. These spells can open doors by removing fear and increasing our willingness to take risks, which lead to success. Attracting good fortune by consecrating a lucky amulet such as a coin or gemstone are common good-luck spells.

Throughout this chapter, we mention things like amulets and sigils. To be sure that you know what each means, we want to give you a quick understanding of them. A charm is almost anything that may be used to attract good luck (i.e., a lucky charm). An amulet is worn for protection. They are believed to have the power to ward off negative energy, evil spirits, or illness. A talisman is used to attract something specific to the owner. A talisman must be consecrated and charged with magickal power by the person preparing it, in order to fill that individual with the specific power and energy of its intended use. A sigil is a symbol or graphical representation that is charged with magickal intent. (There will be a section below explaining how to create your own sigil.) The creation of a sigil typically involves the combination of various symbols, letters, and shapes into a unique design, which is meant to represent a specific desire or intention. Once the sigil is created, it is charged with energy through various means, such as visualization or ritual. Then it is released into the universe to manifest the desired outcome.

CREATING A SACRED SPACE

Because your home should be a sacred space, let's begin with something that will help you to create that sacred space. What you will need are sage and some noisemakers (bells, maracas, drums, etc.). This is a fun activity to do with more others; however, it works just as well to do it by yourself. In the pagan world, most spells depend on timing and intention. This sacred-space cleanse is best to start when the moon is waxing (getting bigger). It is also best to do this three times (as with most spells).

Start this sacred-space cleanse at the entrance of your home with your sage in one hand and your noisemaker in the other. Start walking (counterclockwise) through your home. As you go, make noise. (Ring the bells, clap your hands, etc.) State out loud what you want to leave (negativity, illness, lies, enemies, negative energy, etc.). Once you have gone through every room, go back to the entrance. Now, walk in clockwise circles. While using your noisemakers and sage again, invite what you want in your home (love, abundance, passion, etc.). After going through each room and walking in clockwise circles, go back to the point of entry (your doorway). Open some windows and leave your home for at least thirteen minutes. Then when you come back, you will likely notice that your home will feel differently.

We also encourage you to create your own sigil and place it under your doormat. Another option is bay leaves. Bay leaves are incredible. They remove negative energy and prevent that type of energy from entering when they are hung or placed around the edges of a door. You can tuck them into the upper corners of a doorway, and negative energy will be unable to enter.

BLACK SALT

Witches' Salt is very powerful for protecting, cursing, hexing, binding, and cleansing. You can add black salt to spell jars, protection sachets, poppets, etc. You can sprinkle it in doorways or driveways to help with protection. You can keep a bag in your car or near your bed to ward away nightmares. So we are going to explain to you how to make your own black salt. You will need one cup of sea salt, ash from incense, black pepper, and dried and crushed eggshells. First, finely crush the eggshells in a mortar and pestle. Add the sea salt, ash, and pepper. Blend well. Transfer the contents to a jar.

MOON WATER

There is both new-moon water and full-moon water. To make either, place sterilized water in a sterilized, airtight container. Leave the container out under the new or full moon. The new and full moons are either new or full for three days. So let's say that there is a full moon on October 31. The container should be left outside overnight on October 30 and 31 and November 1.

CORD-CUTTING CEREMONY

Have you ever wanted to cut a toxic person out of your life? Well, here's an easy way to do that. It's called a cord-cutting ceremony. This spell will help break the bonds that hold you to a certain person so that you are able to move on. Here's what you'll need: one white beeswax candle, one black beeswax candle, a black ribbon or string, scissors, and something to write on the candles with (needle, knife, etc.).

Carve your name on the white candle and the name of the person you wish to break ties with on the black candle. Tie the two candles together with the ribbon or string. Make sure to leave space between the two candles so you can cut the ribbon easily. Do not put the ribbon too close to the wick, or it will burn.

Light the candles and chant the following: "These two flames burn brightly together, but one consumes the other with this link between them. No more shall I suffer from the sadness brought by [other person's name]. No more shall I be hurt by [other person's name]. [Other person's name], I sever my ties with thee!"

Cut the ribbon. Let the candles burn out safely—don't leave them unattended. Dispose of the candles separately.

BANISHING OIL

Use this oil to get a candle ready to banish someone or something harmful from your life. You will need

1 teaspoon rosemary
1 teaspoon sage
1 teaspoon black pepper
1 teaspoon cayenne pepper
1 teaspoon cinnamon
2 glass jars with lids

2 ounces olive oil or oil of your choice
Cheesecloth

Place herbs in jar and cover jar with the oil. Place lid on the jar and allow it to sit for a week, shaking the jar daily. Use cheesecloth or something similar to strain oil. Place oil in other glass jar.

ENERGY-CLEARING SPRAY

You may use this spray to clear a room of negative energy or to spray your hands and arms before, during, or after energy sessions. Get a four-ounce spray bottle and fill it most of the way with distilled water. Add a half-teaspoon of real or Himalayan salt, ten drops of lavender oil, ten drops of lemon oil, ten drops of sage oil, ten drops of cedar oil, and one-fourth teaspoon of glycerin. Add a small chip of amethyst or other protecting crystal of your choice. Shake the bottle well before using it.

BAY-LEAF MAGICK

As we stated earlier, bay leaves carry an incredible amount of energy and magick. Here is a quick magick ritual to manifest an intention. You will need three dried bay leaves, a candle, tweezers, and a pencil. Light the candle. Write your intention (what you wish to manifest) on a bay leaf. Hold your hands over the bay leaf and visualize what you wish to manifest. Take the bay leaf with the tweezers and hold the leaf over the candle a little above the flame. Watch to see how quickly the flame reaches the bay leaf. Take note of how much of the bay leaf burns. As the bay leaf burns, place it on a plate or in a bowl. Can you see anything within the leaf as it burns? Do this three times. By the third time, the leaf should burn rather quickly and in its entirety. You may use the ashes in a sachet or necklace, let the wind take them away, or bury them.

BINDING A BULLY

This spell will not cause harm to a bully. It will just make him or her leave you alone. For the greatest effect, complete the spell at midnight on a Saturday while the moon is waning (getting smaller). You will need

- Three black beeswax candles
- Black thread
- A black pen
- A piece of paper
- An empty glass jar with a tightly fitting lid

Set the candles in a triangle. Make sure that the triangle is large enough so that you are able to sit in the middle. Light the candles. Write the bully's name on the paper and draw a large X over the name. Fold the paper three times. Chant the following: "I bind you [name] so that you cannot hurt me anymore, physically and emotionally. Get out of my life and leave me alone. I bind you [name]. I bind you."

Tie the thread around the folded paper and place it in the jar. Snuff out the candles and add the stubs of the candles to the jar. Screw on the lid. Hide or bury the jar far from your property.

EGG CLEANSE

An egg cleanse is a traditional spiritual practice, which involves using a raw egg to remove negative energy or spiritual blockages from a person's body or energy field. For an egg cleanse, you need a fresh egg (at room temperature) and one clear cup or bowl filled with moon water. (See the spell for moon water above.) Hold the egg in your hand and try to place yourself in a meditative state. This can be done by altering your breathing. Breathe in for seven seconds, hold it for seven seconds, and breathe out for seven seconds. Breathe in for eight seconds, hold it for eight seconds, and breathe out for eight seconds.

Breathe in for nine seconds, hold it for nine seconds, and breathe out for nine seconds. Place the egg at your crown chakra and make your way down to your root chakra. Then outline your body with the egg. When you feel ready, crack the egg into the water. Put the shell aside and give the egg time to settle. (Wait at least fifteen minutes.) Then read your egg. Do not look down into the glass because then you will breathe back in any of the negativity that the cleanse captured. Here are some egg-cleanse meanings:

- If there's blood in your egg cleanse, it means you are carrying a lot of heavy negativity, which could result in illness.
- If the water turns cloudy, you must conduct another cleanse because you aren't fully cleansed yet.
- If the water and egg are clear and bubbles are rising to the surface of the water, you're clear of negativity.

Here are some additional meanings:

- Cloudy water and bubbles rising = There is negativity.
- Figures in the yolk = Someone is envious of you.
- Nails or needle shapes = Someone does not want you to succeed, and he or she is working against you.
- Coating on the yolk = Someone is angering you.
- Red or black spots on the yolk = There is disease or illness
- Cloudy, black, or gray yolk = Evil is near.
- White halos around the yolk = You are making decisions too quickly.
- Clouds or swirling figures in the yolk = You are having emotional difficulties.
- Cobwebs = People are wanting you to fail.
- Bubbles around the yolk = Good spirits are around you and want to assist you.

Once you are finished, flush your egg down the toilet.

SIGIL MAKING

As explained above, sigils are magickal symbols used to create change. They can also be used to promote healing and growth or to attract things like money. But they can also be used to curse or banish negative energies. Sigils are diverse tools. Once you learn how to make them, they are quick and effective works of magick.

Sigils work by putting energy behind a specified intent. Intent is represented by a statement, which is transformed into a symbol. It is then charged with energy to fuel the manifestation of your intent. Traditionally, the sigil is charged and then left alone. However, many people have found that keeping the sigil and charging it every once in a while, is just as effective.

An easy way for beginners to create and charge a sigil is to draw a symbol on a piece of paper. The symbol should reflect what you are attempting to manifest. Once the symbol has been drawn, fill it with energy. (The transcriptionist uses her hands by placing them over the symbol.) You can charge it through emotions and sensations, or you may use a crystal that represents what you are manifesting. (Different crystals carry different intentions.) You can also charge it by leaving it under the moon or sun. Much like the bay-leaf magick described above, you may also burn the paper after directing your intentions into the sigil.

SPELL JARS

Spell jars are fun and easy. You are able to create quick go-to jars for spell work. The ingredients should be added as to how you feel they are needed. (The importance of these jars is the ingredients that are added.)

- Prosperity: cinnamon, clove, mint, chamomile, citrine, green aventurine, coins, and green sealing wax
- Happiness: honeysuckle, lemon balm, marjoram, Saint John's wart, carnelian, sunstone, and yellow sealing wax

- Insight: mugwort, bay leaf, sweetgrass, moonstone, labradorite, lapis, and purple sealing wax
- Banishing: cayenne pepper, black pepper, garlic, rosemary, rue, black tourmaline, jet, and black or grey sealing wax
- Love: rose, jasmine, lavender, basil, pink salt (Himalayan pink salt to protect relationships and remove negative blockages and curses), rose quartz, garnet, and pink sealing wax
- Healing: lavender, calendula, eucalyptus, turmeric, amethyst, clear quartz, sea salt, and blue sealing wax
- Success: lemon balm, bergamot, cinnamon, ginger, tiger's eye, pyrite, citrine, and gold sealing wax
- Protection: angelica, nettle, lavender, bay leaf, obsidian, smoky quartz, black salt, and black sealing wax

BIBLIOMANCY

It's common for some witches to open a magickal tome at random as a means of divination. Basically, divination is based on the first word or sentence that their eyes focus on. There is a subtlety to this practice, which some do not know about or have forgotten. And this subtlety ensures magickal success. The consulted book must have fallen down from the shelf on its own. Only a book that presents itself of its own accord will be wholly reliable for consultation. Here is the procedure:

1. Once a book has fallen, pick it up respectfully, dust it off gently, and hold it to your heart for several moments.
2. Place the book on a table, balanced on its spine.
3. Allow the pages to fall open.
4. Close your eyes and place your finger on the open pages.
5. Allow your finger to move across and around the pages until it seems to stop on its own.
6. Open your eyes to see what word or sentence your finger has selected.

TAROT-CARD TRICKS

Tarot cards are one of the main forms of divination that witches use. However, there are some quick tricks that even a beginner may use.

- If you're feeling nervous about a situation, shuffle your tarot deck and look for the Fool. The two cards on either side will advise you on how to approach it.
- If you're doing some soul-searching, shuffle your tarot deck and find The Hermit. The cards around him will shed some light on your introspection.
- If you're going through some major life changes, shuffle your tarot deck and find The World. The cards around it will give you the advice you need for this new chapter.

SUBSTITUTIONS

Sometimes you may find that you just can't locate all the items that you need in the middle of spell work. Here are some quick substitutions that could work:

- Clear quartz can replace any crystal.
- White candles can replace any color of candle.
- Rosemary can replace any herb.
- A rose can replace any flower.
- Frankincense or copal can replace any resin.
- Tobacco can replace any poisonous herb.

This chapter is close to coming to an end. In closing, we are going to leave you with the knowledge of a few magickal herbs and their uses (and then some quick witchy tips).

MAGICKAL HERBS AND THEIR USES

- Ginger: protection from evil
- Garlic: repelling thieves and blessing a new home
- Chili: spells for fidelity and sex magic
- Nutmeg: combats rheumatism, colds, neuralgia, and eye sties
- Cloves: exorcism, healing, love, and money
- Bok choy: banishment and protection
- Cinnamon: abundance, wealth, money, riches, and prosperity
- Capers: romance, fertility, and abundance
- Star anise: power, generation, and psychic visions
- Pepper: courage and warding off jealousy
- Rosemary: past-life recall and psychic detox
- Thyme: good luck and protection from evil
- Allspice: relieving aches
- Vanilla: peace and tranquility
- Cardamom: clarity, courage, direction, and wisdom
- Chives: breaking hexes and love magic
- Mint: protection, money, and healing
- Rocket or arugula: fertility and health

And as promised, here are some quick witchy tips:

- Save your hair and burn it on a full moon.
- Stir your coffee clockwise and draw a pentagram in it.
- When you come out of the shower, and the mirrors are damp, draw a protection sigil on them. See above for how to make your own sigil or can use this one for protection:

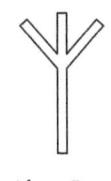

Algiz Rune

It is known as the Algiz (or Elhaz) rune. It is an ancient runic symbol that was used by Germanic and Nordic tribes. It is associated with the god Heimdallr, who is the guardian of the gods in Norse mythology. The shape of the Algiz rune resembles the shape of the human hand, with the index finger and little finger raised and the other fingers folded inward. This makes it a symbol of protection and defense as well as a symbol of connection to the divine. The Algiz rune is often used in modern-day runic divination and magical practices. In divination, it is believed to represent protection, defense, and spiritual guidance. In magick, it is used for protective spells, as well as for invoking the power and guidance of the gods.

- Save rainwater and charge it under the full moon.
- Draw sigils under your shoes.
- Leave milk and honey in a dish out under the full moon for your friendly house spirits.

With that, my dears, our chapter is done. You will likely see us again (if you want). We are working on a book with many more witch tips and practices. Until then, we hope you find the magick in life.

COMMENTARY BY ANUBIS

Thank you, Hekate and The Witch. This chapter was so much fun to read and be a part of. They are indeed working on another book with this transcriptionist, and it promises to not only be magickal but also filled with so much knowledge that your everyday life will feel magickal (just as it should feel). Now, this next chapter is written by Quetzalcoatl. Quetzalcoatl is a Mesoamerican deity, who was worshiped by the Aztecs, Mayans, Toltecs, and other ancient civilizations in Mexico and Central America. His name means feathered serpent, which is a common symbol in Mesoamerican mythology and art. In mythology, Quetzalcoatl is a god of creation, fertility, wisdom, and knowledge. He is often depicted as a serpent with feathers or as a man with a serpent's head. It is associated with the wind, the morning star, and the planet Venus. According to legend, Quetzalcoatl was responsible for creating humanity and bringing civilization to the people. He taught them agriculture, astronomy, art, and other skills. He was seen as a benevolent god who cared for his people. After the arrival of the Spanish in the sixteenth century, Quetzalcoatl was equated with the Christian figure of Saint Thomas and was seen by some as a symbol of resistance against the conquistadors. This chapter will be most interesting, as it seems that he will guide you to your very own dragon.

CHAPTER 9

QUETZALCOATL

I have been waiting very patiently for my turn. And I am so excited to begin. Please note that this is the only chapter that has a prerequisite. For me to be your guide, you must have intentionally picked this chapter. There is a ritual that you must recall. It is likely that you never performed this ritual if you did not intentionally pick this chapter.

To start, I am an energy that some humans have never heard of. Yet I am also an energy that humans in various areas of the Earth worship regularly. It is wonderful to be able to reach people who would otherwise not know of me. Also, I want to tell you that the transcriptionist would have chosen my chapter to begin with (as she is linked to the number nine).

The number nine is a significant number in many cultures and belief systems around the world. It has been associated with various meanings and symbols. Here are a few examples.

1. Completion and Wholeness

In numerology, which is the study of the mystical meanings of numbers, the number nine is considered a symbol of completion and wholeness. It is the last single-digit number, and therefore, it represents the end of a cycle.

2. Enlightenment

In Buddhism, the Buddha is said to have taught nine ways of meditation, which lead to enlightenment. Therefore, the number nine is considered a symbol of spiritual attainment and awakening.

3. Creativity and Vision

In Hinduism, the number nine is associated with the goddess Saraswati, who is the patron of knowledge, creativity, and the arts. It is believed that invoking her energy can bring forth creative inspiration and vision.

4. Unity and Oneness

In Christianity, the Holy Trinity is made up of three divine persons, but it is also said to be one entity. When the number nine is multiplied by any number, the digits of the resulting number will always add up to nine, which is seen as a symbol of the unity and oneness of God.

5. Universal Love

In astrology, the number nine is associated with the planet Neptune, which is said to govern universal love and compassion. The number nine is also associated with the heart chakra, which is the energy center in the body associated with love, compassion, and empathy.

Overall, the number nine is a powerful symbol, which is associated with completion, wholeness, spiritual attainment, creativity, unity, and love. Its significance varies depending on the cultural and spiritual context it is used in.

In tarot, the number nine is associated with the Major Arcana card called "The Hermit." The transcriptionist is a number nine. This card depicts a solitary figure holding a lantern and standing on a mountain. This represents the search for inner wisdom and spiritual enlightenment. Here are some of the key meanings and symbolism associated with the number nine in the Tarot.

1. Reflection and Introspection

The Hermit represents the need to turn inward and reflect on one's own thoughts, feelings, and experiences. It is a time to withdraw from the external world and seek inner guidance and wisdom.

2. Spiritual Awakening

The Hermit is also associated with spiritual enlightenment and the discovery of one's true purpose in life. The lantern held by the Hermit represents the light of knowledge that illuminates the path of self-discovery.

3. Patience and Perseverance

The Hermit suggests that the journey to self-discovery is a long and often difficult one, requiring patience and perseverance. It may involve facing fears, overcoming obstacles, and letting go of old patterns and beliefs.

4. Wisdom and Guidance

The Hermit is often seen as a wise and knowledgeable figure, who can offer guidance and support to those who seek it. His presence in a Tarot reading may suggest the need to seek out a mentor or spiritual teacher who can provide insight and wisdom.

Overall, the number nine in the Tarot is associated with the search for inner wisdom and spiritual enlightenment and the need to withdraw from the external world in order to focus on one's own growth and development. She is transcribing this book as part of her life journey as a number nine. After this life, she will no longer need to continue learning about anything as a human. This is her final journey as a human (if she wishes it to be). That is the significance of the number nine.

So if you have picked this number, you are likely someone who is very open to messages from the universe. You have come far in your journey into spiritual awakening. You are likely connected to the heartbeat and spirit of the multiverse. Connecting with me is therefore relatively simple for you. If you are having difficulty connecting with me, let me give you a little more background about myself. As Anubis stated, I was worshiped by the Aztecs, Mayans, Toltecs, and other ancient civilizations in Mexico and Central America. The Aztecs built temples and shrines to honor me. One of the most famous sites associated with my worship is the Pyramid of the Sun, which is located near modern-day Mexico City. This pyramid was built around 200 AD. Here is a picture of it:

Pyramid of the Sun at Teotihuacan

Teotihuacan was one of the largest and most influential cities in Mesoamerica. The Pyramid of the Sun is one of the most impressive and well-known structures at the site. The pyramid is constructed of stone and Earth, and it is thought to have been built using traditional Mesoamerican construction techniques. It stands approximately seventy-five meters tall, making it one of the largest pyramids in Mesoamerica.

The pyramid is located at the center of the Teotihuacan complex. It is surrounded by other important structures and monuments. It is characterized by a series of terraces, which lead up to the summit. These terraces are divided by steps, which are marked with stone carvings and intricate patterns. The summit of the pyramid is a flat platform, which is thought to have been used for ceremonial purposes. One of the most fascinating features of the Pyramid of the Sun is its orientation. The pyramid is aligned with cardinal directions. Its western side faces the setting sun.

Now, close your eyes and picture yourself at this pyramid. Perhaps you have already been there in a past life. Or perhaps (if you know the location), you are able to project your consciousness to this pyramid. Climb the stairs and walk into the pyramid. Smell the air and dirt. Perhaps you are able to feel the stones and the consciousness of the pyramid. Once you are comfortable with this vision of yourself inside the pyramid, look toward the entrance. You will see me entering. I will know whether you are comfortable seeing me or not, and I will alter my appearance to ensure that you are not alarmed. While many humans are fascinated with the idea of dragons, actually seeing one could be jarring to some of you (especially if you have never encountered one before). Whenever you wish to connect with me, take this journey into the pyramid and ask me to be there.

Another way to connect with me is to create an altar or a shrine. To do this, choose a space in your home that feels sacred to you and decorate it with images and symbols associated with me, such as feathers, snakes, or the colors red and white. Presenting an offering is also a possibility. An offering may include flowers, incense, food, or objects that have special meaning to you. Here are some of the most commonly recognized symbols and objects connected to me.

1. Feathered Serpent

The feathered serpent (or dragon) is perhaps the most recognizable symbol associated with me. It is a combination of two powerful symbols—the serpent and the bird—and it represents the duality of nature, as well as the idea of transformation and renewal.

2. Wind

I am often associated with the wind, which is a symbol of the life force and breath of creation. I am sometimes depicted with a conch shell, which I use to summon the winds and communicate with the gods.

3. Maize

In Mesoamerican culture, maize (corn) was an important symbol of life and sustenance. I was sometimes associated with maize. (I taught humans how to cultivate it.)

4. Jade

Jade was a precious and highly valued stone in Mesoamerican culture. It was often used to make jewelry and other decorative objects. I am sometimes depicted wearing a jade headdress or necklace, which symbolizes my connection to the natural world.

5. Morning Star

I am often associated with the planet Venus, which is known as the morning star. This celestial connection reinforces my association with the sky and heavens.

Once you have connected with me, it will be easy for you to invoke me. My gift is to connect you with a dragon. This dragon will (as in the chapter before mine) help you to understand that magick is in everyday life and that there are realms beyond yours. If you wish, this dragon will meet you as your consciousness transmutes (i.e., when this body of yours is no longer able to sustain your human life). Since dragons are magickal beings, and they have been hidden from humans for ages, you will have to recall a detailed ritual before connecting with your guardian dragon. While that ritual must be labeled as a blood ritual, you will not actually be performing a blood ritual. This is because you have already completed this blood ritual in a past life.

A blood ritual typically refers to a ritualistic practice where blood is used as a symbolic or actual medium for a certain purpose, such as making a sacrifice, invoking supernatural powers, or establishing a bond or covenant. Blood rituals have been practiced by various cultures throughout history, and they can take many forms. In some cases, blood is drawn from participants and is used in symbolic ways, such as painting symbols or words on objects or surfaces. In other cases, blood is spilled or is offered as a sacrifice, either as a symbolic gesture or as a means of appeasing deities or supernatural forces.

Again, you will not actually be performing a blood ritual; you are going to remember or recall a blood ritual that you have already performed. Because you chose this chapter, you had already conducted a blood ritual for this exact purpose in a past life. I want to make one thing clear: For me to be your guide, you must have intentionally picked this chapter. So this chapter is very different from the other chapters and guides. Like the transcriptionist, without even knowing who the guides are within this book, you must have picked this chapter and the number nine automatically and intentionally.

To recall your covenant with me and my realm, you may do a specific meditation. You will be introduced to your guardian dragon through an astral-projection session. The transcriptionist was shown her guardian dragon during an astral-projection session. I will explain that meditation now.

Prepare yourself for this meditation by finding a comfortable position, either seated or lying down, and gently closing your eyes. Take a deep breath in, allowing the air to fill your lungs, and exhale slowly, releasing any tension or distractions from the outside world. With each breath, let your body relax. Feel the weight of your body sinking into the surface beneath you.

Next, imagine yourself standing in a lush, vibrant forest, surrounded by towering trees and the sweet scent of nature. Feel the gentle warmth of the sun on your skin and a soft breeze brushing against your face. You are safe and protected in this sacred space.

As you walk deeper into the forest, you notice a glimmer of light dancing through the leaves. Follow this radiant light as it leads you to a clearing, where I await. I'm adorned in magnificent feathers that shimmer with my every movement. My presence will emanate a sense of tranquility and wisdom. Approach me with reverence and humility, knowing that you are in the presence of an ancient and powerful guide. I welcome you with open arms. I invite you to sit or kneel beside me.

Take a moment to connect with my energy. Feel my serpentine wisdom and vitality flowing through your being. Allow my divine essence to merge with your own, creating a harmonious union of energies.

Now, envision yourself surrounded by a brilliant golden light, which symbolizes the sacred wisdom bestowed upon you by me. With each breath, visualize this radiant light expanding within you as it illuminates every cell of your body and infuses your mind, heart, and soul with clarity and serenity.

As you bask in my divine presence, allow any thoughts or worries to gently fade away. Surrender to the stillness within and let go of any attachments or limitations that hold you back. Feel a deep sense of inner peace and liberation filling your entire being.

In this state of tranquility, ask me to grant you the guidance and wisdom to recall your covenant. Trust that the answers and insights you seek will be revealed to you. Take a few moments to express your gratitude to me. Feel the immense love and compassion emanating from me to you, knowing that you are always supported and protected.

As the meditation comes to a close, slowly bring your awareness back to the present moment. Feel the ground beneath you and gently open your eyes. Carry the wisdom and serenity of this meditation. Remember, my essence resides within you, and you may tap into my divine energy whenever you seek guidance, balance, and connection with the sacred.

Since you have already conducted a blood ritual to be able to enter my realm, many of you may have already encountered a dragon. (This or these dragons may or may not end up being your guardians). Encountering an actual dragon is something that you will never forget. While there are countless variations and interpretations of dragons in different cultures, here are some notable ones.

1. Western Dragon

The western dragon is one of the most well-known types. It typically has four legs, a pair of wings, and a long serpentine body. Western dragons are often associated with European folklore, and they are portrayed as powerful creatures who guard treasures.

2. Eastern Dragon

The eastern dragon, commonly found in Chinese and other East Asian mythologies, differs significantly from its western counterpart. These dragons are long serpentine creatures with no wings. They are revered as benevolent and wise beings associated with water and rain.

3. Wyverns

Wyverns are dragon-like creatures with two legs and a pair of wings. Unlike western dragons, wyverns do not have front limbs, and their wings function as their front limbs. They often have a scorpion-like tail with a venomous stinger. Wyverns are commonly depicted in European folklore and heraldry.

4. Amphipteres

The amphiptere is a type of dragon that lacks legs or claws. (The transcriptionist has met this type of dragon.) It has a serpent-like body and wings, and it is sometimes adorned with feathers. Amphipteres are often associated with heraldic symbolism. They can be found in European mythology and medieval art.

5. Lindworms

The Lindworm is a dragon-like creature that appears in Norse and Germanic folklore. It is depicted as a serpent-like creature with two front limbs and no hind legs. Lindworms are usually depicted as fierce and malevolent creatures.

6. Hydras

The Hydra is a multiheaded dragon-like creature from Greek mythology. It has the ability to regrow two heads for each one that is severed. Hydras are usually depicted as water-dwelling creatures and are known for their poisonous breath.

7. Drakes

Drakes are smaller and are less powerful dragons when compared to their larger counterparts. They are often depicted with two or four legs and wings.

Their temperament and abilities can vary in different mythologies and fantasy settings.

8. Elemental Dragons

Elemental dragons are associated with the classical elements of fire, water, air, and Earth. (The transcriptionist has met an Earth dragon.) They embody and control their respective elements, and they are often depicted as immensely powerful beings. These dragons can vary in appearance and abilities based on their elemental affiliation.

9. Celestial Dragons

Celestial dragons are often depicted as celestial beings. They reside in the heavens or other celestial realms. (The transcriptionist has also met this type of dragon.) They are associated with cosmic powers and are sometimes portrayed as benevolent guardians or wise guides.

10. Dragonets

Dragonets, also known as dragonlings or baby dragons, are the young offspring of dragons. They are smaller and less powerful than adult dragons and often lack certain abilities, such as the ability to breathe fire. Dragonets are sometimes portrayed as mischievous or playful creatures.

These are just a few examples of the different types of dragons found in mythology and fantasy literature. Each type has its own unique characteristics, appearances, and cultural significance.

For me to introduce you to your guardian dragon, you will need to do so through a specific astral-projection session. Although chapter two describes one way to travel the astral plane, that explanation is specifically connected to Xia's exercise. I am going to explain how to generally enter that plane.

Astral projection, also known as an out-of-body experience (OBE), is the practice of intentionally separating your consciousness or spirit from your physical body and allowing it to explore other realms or dimensions. Here are some general steps to help you enter an astral-projection state.

1. Prepare Your Environment

Find a quiet and comfortable space where you won't be disturbed. Dim the lights or create a calming atmosphere. Some people prefer to play soft, soothing music or to use incense or essential oils to aid relaxation.

2. Relaxation and Meditation

Start by relaxing your body and mind through deep breathing and progressive muscle relaxation. Lie down or sit in a comfortable position, close your eyes, and focus on your breath. Allow any tension or stress to melt away as you enter a meditative state.

3. Reach a Deeply Relaxed State

Once you feel calm and relaxed, continue with meditation techniques to deepen your state of relaxation. You can use visualization, mindfulness, or any other meditation method that works for you. The goal is to achieve a state of deep relaxation while remaining alert and aware.

4. Intention and Visualization

Set a clear intention to separate your consciousness from your physical body. Visualize yourself floating or rising above your body and seeing it from a different perspective. Imagine yourself being light, free, and ready to explore the astral realm.

5. Separation Techniques

There are several techniques that you can use to facilitate the separation of your consciousness from your body. Some popular methods include:

- The rope technique: Visualize a rope hanging above you. Mentally reach out and grab the rope, feeling its texture. Imagine yourself pulling your astral body upward and gently separating it from your physical body.
- The rollout technique: Visualize yourself lying on a surface. Imagine yourself rolling over and feeling your astral body separate and detach from your physical body.
- Energy visualization: Visualize your body filled with vibrant, glowing energy. Focus on this energy expanding, lifting you out of your physical body, and allowing your astral form to separate.

6. Maintain Focus and Awareness

As you attempt to separate, it's important to remain focused and to maintain a clear and alert state of mind. Avoid falling asleep or losing concentration. You can use affirmations or repeated mantras to stay focused on your intention.

7. Explore the Astral Realm

Once you feel separated from your physical body, you can explore the astral realm. It's important to stay calm and open-minded during this experience. You can visit different locations, meet entities, or simply observe your surroundings. Remember to maintain your intention and focus to avoid getting too caught up in the experience.

8. Return to Your Body

When you're ready to end the astral projection, simply set the intention to return to your physical body. Visualize yourself descending or floating back into your body and gradually reconnecting with your physical sensations. Take some time to integrate and reflect on your experience.

If you have never entered the astral plane, and you are going to attempt for the first time (in this lifetime), please request that I be your guide and/or guardian. It is important for you to have a gatekeeper. A gatekeeper refers to a spiritual entity or energy that serves as a guardian or intermediary between the diviner and the realm of the divine or the spiritual realm. The gatekeeper facilitates communication and access to the information, guidance, or messages sought during the divination process. A gatekeeper acts as a protector and guide, ensuring that the divination process remains safe, accurate, and respectful. The role of a gatekeeper can vary, but generally, they are responsible for the following.

1. Opening and Closing the Spiritual Gate

Gatekeepers create a connection or portal between the diviner and the spiritual realm. They open the gate at the beginning of the divination process and allow access to the desired information or guidance. At the end of the session, they close the gate and ensure a proper conclusion to the spiritual connection.

2. Providing Protection

Gatekeepers are often seen as protective entities who safeguard the diviner from negative or unwanted spiritual influences or energies. They create a safe space for the divination process and shield the diviner from any potential harm or interference.

3. Acting as an Intermediary

Gatekeepers serve as intermediaries between the diviner and the spiritual realm. They facilitate communication and interaction with the divine, spirits, ancestors, or other entities. They may assist in translating or interpreting messages that are received during the divination process.

4. Maintaining Sacred Boundaries

Gatekeepers help establish and maintain the sacredness and integrity of the divination space. They ensure that the spiritual realm and its energies are respected. They guide the diviner in conducting the practice appropriately and ethically.

Many of you already have several gatekeepers. Please feel free to use any of them upon entering my realm. You may also use me as your gatekeeper (once your gatekeepers have confirmed my identity). Now let's look at the meditation that will enable you to enter my realm and meet your guardian dragon.

Once you are on the astral plane, picture yourself standing on the edge of a towering mountain peak and feeling the crisp air brushing against your skin. As you gaze out into the horizon, a sense of anticipation fills your being.

Sense the shift in energy around you as I emerge from the depths of the sky. When I descend on the mountaintop, you sense that I bring the radiant energy of ancient knowledge.

With utmost reverence and trust, I will approach you and extend my hand. As you take my hand, a portal of swirling energy opens, revealing my hidden realm. To enter the portal, you must speak the words that you spoke during your blood ritual. (You might remember these words in a different language.) Those words will allow you to enter my realm.

As you step through the portal, a majestic dragon greets you with a dignified presence. Its scales shimmer, reflecting the profound power it embodies. This dragon is a being of immense wisdom and ancient lineage and a guardian of arcane secrets.

As I am the bridge between worlds, I introduce you to the dragon with a deep understanding of the connection between humans and these mythical creatures. Through their translation, you are able to perceive the dragon's thoughts and intentions, establishing a sacred and profound communication.

Feel the dragon's energy envelop you. It's a potent mix of strength, grace, and profound insight. As you bask in its presence, you become aware of the boundless knowledge that resides within this creature, which was accumulated throughout countless ages.

The dragon, guided by me, imparts wisdom and secrets of the universe, which transcend human understanding. Listen attentively to its ancient voice and feel the resonance of its words deep within your soul. Allow the dragon's wisdom to ignite the dormant knowledge within you, unlock your hidden potential, and expand your consciousness.

In this moment of union between you, me, and the dragon, you recognize the interwoven tapestry of existence. You become aware that within you lies the essence of the dragon—a divine spark waiting to be awakened. When you feel that spark, you will receive the name that your dragon wishes to be called by you.

Express your gratitude to the dragon for this profound encounter, knowing that the wisdom shared will guide and shape your path. As you bid farewell to the dragon, step back through the portal and feel the energies of the mystical realm gently recede.

Return to the present moment, knowing that the bond forged with the dragon will continue to resonate within you. Carry this sacred connection as a reminder of the eternal mysteries that exist beyond the veil of ordinary perception and inspire you to seek higher truths and embrace the limitless possibilities of your own existence.

You may feel different after this meditation. Having not only entered my realm (in this lifetime) but also having the knowledge of dragons creates new pathways within your mind, which enable you to open yourself up to a more peaceful existence and the ability to climb the ladder of transcendence. Use this meditation and these techniques to meet with your guardian dragon regularly. This will establish your relationship with him or her and deepen your connection with each other. Your guardian dragon will also likely wish to take you to other realms within the multiverse (once establishing a deeper connection with you).

I hope you have enjoyed this chapter. I have very much enjoyed meeting all of you who have chosen to read my chapter and reenter my realm. My wish for humanity is that you are all able to progress and that you have a much better understanding of how magical life can be.

COMMENTARY BY ANUBIS

Thank you, Quetzalcoatl. Your participation in this book is exciting, and the ability to travel to the dragon realm is such a gift. I know the transcriptionist felt blessed to know that you were to be the author of the chapter she would have picked. The next guide is Enki, the Sumerian god of water, knowledge, crafts, and creation. This next chapter may be considered controversial to some humans because Enki is also one of the Anunnaki. There are several different theories about what (and who) the Anunnaki are. As Enki will explain, the Anunnaki are otherworldly beings. Before you make any judgments (as could have been done with chapter two), please take some time to read Enki's chapter. It is enlightening, and it will explain how to discover your purpose for being here in this lifetime (and why and how your life connects with the purpose of your divine self).

CHAPTER 10

ENKI

I am Enki. I was an important deity in the mythology of ancient Mesopotamia, specifically in the Sumerian and Akkadian civilizations. I am one of their major gods. I played a central role in the creation of humanity and the establishment of civilization. As Anubis stated, I was associated with water, wisdom, crafts, magic, and fertility.

In Sumerian mythology, I am known as Ea, the son of the god Anu, who is the ruler of the heavens. My mother is Nammu, a primordial goddess associated with primeval waters. I have often been portrayed as a wise and benevolent deity, who is responsible for the creation of humankind. According to Sumerian myths, I played a crucial role in the development of civilization by providing knowledge, technology, and laws to humanity. I am also associated with the city of Eridu, which is considered one of the oldest cities in Mesopotamia. It was my main center of worship.

In Akkadian mythology, I am known as Ea. In the Akkadian tradition, I am depicted as a more powerful and influential deity. Ea was considered the patron god of magic and sorcery and was associated with the freshwater sources, particularly rivers and streams. I am often depicted as a bearded figure, which is wearing a horned crown and holding a scepter or a bucket of water. These symbolize my dominion over the watery realms.

I have also been known for my involvement in various myths and legends. One well-known myth is the *Enuma Elish*, the Babylonian creation epic, in which I played a significant role in the formation of the world and the establishment of order. In another myth known as *The Atrahasis Epic*, I aided humanity by helping them survive a great flood, which had been sent by the gods to wipe them (humanity) out. I advised a mortal hero named Atrahasis to build an ark and save both humans and animals.

Before delving into the Anunnaki and our relationship with humans, I would like to first discuss the number ten and its meaning for purposes of this book and chapter because this is the first chapter in this book to have two numbers (one and zero).

In numerology, the number ten is considered a powerful and significant number. It is seen as a combination of the energies and vibrations of the numbers one and zero, amplifying their influences.

The number one represents new beginnings, independence, self-confidence, leadership, and ambition. It signifies taking action, assertiveness, and the ability to manifest one's desires. The number zero, on the other hand, represents potential, wholeness, infinite possibilities, and the journey of spiritual growth. It is associated with the qualities of the divine, eternity, and the concept of oneness.

When these energies are combined in the number ten, it represents a cycle of completion and new beginnings. It symbolizes the end of one phase and the start of another, which indicates a transition or transformation. The number ten encourages individuals to embrace change, take risks, and step into their personal power.

In numerology, the number ten is often associated with attributes such as independence, determination, individuality, leadership, innovation, and self-confidence. It suggests that individuals who resonate with this number have the potential to achieve success and manifest their goals through their focused efforts.

Furthermore, the number ten is often seen as a symbol of divine guidance and protection. It can be interpreted as a sign that you are on the right path and that the universe is supporting your endeavors. It encourages you to trust your intuition and embrace the opportunities that come your way.

In the tarot, the number ten holds great significance, as it represents the culmination of a cycle, completion, and new beginnings. It is associated with the final stage of a journey, the lessons learned, and the potential for transformation.

In the traditional Tarot deck, the tenth card of the Major Arcana is known as The Wheel of Fortune. This card depicts a large wheel with various symbols and figures, which represents the ever-turning cycles of life. The Wheel of Fortune embodies the principles of change, luck, and the inevitable ups and downs that one encounters on life's path.

The Wheel-of-Fortune card encourages individuals to embrace the cyclical nature of existence. It reminds one that life is constantly in motion and that everything is subject to change. Just as the wheel turns, the circumstances and experiences of our lives do too. The number ten that is associated with this card signifies the completion of one phase and the beginning of another, which symbolizes a turning point or a significant transition.

The number ten in the Tarot also holds connections to other cards and concepts within the deck. For instance, when adding the digits of ten together (1+0), you arrive at the number one. This connection highlights the cyclical nature of the Tarot, where the completion of one cycle leads to the beginning of another. The number one signifies new beginnings, individuality, and the initiation of a new journey.

Furthermore, the number ten is often linked to the Minor Arcana suit of Cups. In this suit, the Ten of Cups represents emotional fulfillment, harmony, and contentment in relationships. It signifies a sense of completion and satisfaction on an emotional level, indicating that the journey of the heart has reached a fulfilling conclusion.

In a broader metaphysical sense, the number ten represents unity and the concept of oneness. It symbolizes divine connection, harmonious blending of energies, and the realization that all aspects of life are interconnected. It encourages individuals to recognize their places within the larger whole and to seek balance and harmony in their actions.

When the number ten appears in a Tarot reading, it suggests that a cycle is coming to an end and that new opportunities are on the horizon. It signifies a time of completion, closure, and reflection and urges individuals to take stock of their experiences and lessons learned. It invites individuals to embrace change and be open to new beginnings, as the completion of one phase paves the way for fresh possibilities and growth.

In summary, the number ten in the Tarot represents the culmination of a cycle, completion, and new beginnings. It signifies the inevitable nature of change, the interconnectedness of life, and the potential for transformation. Whether encountered in The Wheel of Fortune or the Ten of Cups, this number prompts individuals to reflect on their journeys, embrace change, and seize the opportunities that lie ahead.

With this in mind (the concepts of new beginnings, rebirth, the completion of a cycle), I want to explain a bit about the Anunnaki. The Anunnaki are a group of deities in ancient Mesopotamian mythology, particularly the Sumerian and Akkadian civilizations. The term *Anunnaki* translates to "those who came from heaven to Earth" or "those who from the heavens came down." We have often been portrayed as divine beings with a higher status than humans and possessing immense power and knowledge.

According to Sumerian mythology, we (the Anunnaki) were believed to be the children of Anu, the sky god, and Ki, the Earth goddess. We formed a pantheon of gods and goddesses, who governed different aspects of the world. Among the prominent Anunnaki figures were me (Enki or Ea), Inanna (Ishtar), Ninhursag, Utu (Shamash), and Nanna (Sin). As deities, we held various roles, such as ruling over the heavens, the Earth, the underworld, fertility, war, and wisdom.

We were considered to be intermediaries between the divine and human realms. We were believed to be responsible for the creation of humanity, shaping human civilization, and providing humans with knowledge and guidance.

One well-known story involving the Anunnaki is the *Epic of Gilgamesh*, an ancient Babylonian story. In this tale, the hero Gilgamesh encounters various deities, including the Anunnaki, and embarks on a quest for immortality.

It is important to note that the concept and depiction of the Anunnaki vary across different Mesopotamian texts and periods. In later Babylonian and Assyrian traditions, the Anunnaki were often associated with specific celestial bodies, such as the planets, and were considered more like planetary deities rather than a unified group.

We (the Anunnaki) have garnered significant attention in modern alternative history and conspiracy theories. Some proponents of these theories suggest that we were extraterrestrial beings who visited or influenced ancient Earth's civilizations, attributing advanced knowledge and technology to their interactions with humanity. Along with this concept is the theory that we (the Anunnaki) altered human DNA and genetically manipulated early humans, resulting in the evolution of the human species.

Some humans are appalled and angered by this concept because they believe that we should never have been part of engineering the human species. To this, I ask why it matters. You are who you are. Whether we were part of engineering your species or not, who cares? It seems like some humans are not happy unless they are angry or depressed. Where exactly does that get you in life? It gets you nowhere. If you must get angry about something, why aren't you angry about the loss of civil rights to certain groups or the inhumane treatment of other humans and animals? Perhaps it's because being angry with us means that you don't really have to do anything about it because there is no action to take. And being angry about something that matters means that an action could (and should) be taken to prevent any further loss of civil rights or inhumane treatment of humans and animals. Perhaps being angry about something like this allows you to forget or pretend not to notice the things that should make you want to take action. The biggest problem here is that when you focus on something that you cannot change, it means that you aren't focusing on your purpose for coming here in the first place.

Before continuing, there are two concepts that I would like to explain. Your divine self and the higher self should be differentiated. The divine self is the ultimate, transcendent, or divine aspect of your consciousness or being. It is often associated with a universal or cosmic consciousness, a higher power, or a divine source. Your divine self is the highest, most sacred aspect of your identity. It is inherently connected to the divine or spiritual realm. It is the core essence of who you truly are. It is beyond your ego or physical existence.

Your higher self connects you in this lifetime to your divine self. Your higher self holds your inner wisdom, intuition, and spiritual or moral guidance. It may be thought of as a wiser, more enlightened aspect of your consciousness. Your higher self is tuned into spiritual truths and the greater purpose of life. It can offer guidance and insight to help you make better choices and evolve spiritually. Your higher self is part of your psyche, which may be accessed and developed through self-awareness and spiritual practices.

The key difference between your divine self and higher self lies in their natures and sources. Your divine self is associated with a universal or cosmic source of divine consciousness while your higher self may be seen as an inner, wiser aspect of your consciousness. But both your higher self and divine self involve a deeper, more spiritual understanding of who you are. They just emphasize different aspects of your relationship with the divine or spiritual realm.

So now comes the burning questions. Why are you here? What is the purpose of life? Before your incarnation into this life (and before each incarnation), each and every one of you devised a purpose. Sometimes that purpose is to research so that when your consciousness transmutes, you are able to explain why some humans are more likely to turn away from love and transcendence. Sometimes that purpose is to experience very particular emotions so that you may help and guide others through those same experiences and emotions. For some of you, your purpose may be much more general, and for others, your purpose is much more specific. To connect with that purpose, I am going to guide you through meditations to connect with your higher self and divine self.

Connecting with your higher self through meditation can be a deeply transformative and enlightening experience. Here is a detailed meditation guide to help you establish that connection.

PREPARATION

1. Choose a Quiet Space.

Find a quiet, comfortable space where you won't be disturbed. Sit in a comfortable position, either on a floor cushion or in a chair, with your back straight but not rigid.

2. Set an Intention

Begin by setting a clear intention for your meditation. Here, your intention is to connect with your higher self and to gain insight into your purpose for incarnating into this life. State your intention either silently or aloud.

3. Relaxation

Take a few moments to relax your body and mind. Close your eyes and take a few deep, cleansing breaths. Let go of any tension or stress.

THE MEDITATION

- Grounding: Visualize roots extending from the base of your spine, going deep into the Earth, and anchoring you to the ground. Feel the stability and support of the Earth beneath you.
- Protection: Imagine a bubble of white or golden light surrounding you. This protective barrier will help keep your meditation space safe and free from negative energies.
- Breathing: Focus your attention on your breath. Breathe in slowly through your nose, counting to four, and then exhale through your mouth, also counting to four. Repeat this several times until you feel calm and centered.

- Guided visualization: Imagine yourself walking through a beautiful garden, forest, or any serene place that feels calming to you. As you explore this environment, be aware of the sights, sounds, and sensations around you.
- Encounter your higher self: Eventually, you will come across a door or gate. Open this door or gate with the intention of meeting your higher self. Your higher self might appear as a wise and loving figure or simply as a radiant light.
- Engage in dialogue: Begin a conversation with your higher self. You can ask questions or seek guidance. Your higher self may communicate without words. Trust your intuition and listen carefully to the responses you receive, which may come as words, feelings, or images.
- Receive Insights: Allow your higher self to share insights, wisdom, and guidance with you. Be open to whatever comes, without judgment.
- Integration: Before leaving this meditative state, express gratitude to your higher self for its guidance and wisdom. Express your intention to integrate these insights into your daily life.

CLOSING: RETURN

Slowly begin to return to your awareness of the physical space around you. Visualize yourself walking back through the garden or forest and approaching the door or gate.

- Closing the door or gate: Close the door or gate behind you, leaving a connection to your higher self open for future meditations.
- Grounding and protection: Gradually bring your awareness back to your physical body. Wiggle your fingers and toes and take a few deep breaths. Imagine the protective bubble around you dissipating.
- Reflection: Take a moment to journal your experiences, insights, and any guidance you received during the meditation.

Connecting with your higher self is a personal and individual experience. It may take time and practice to establish a strong and clear connection. Be patient with yourself and approach this meditation with an open heart and mind. Over time, you may find that your connection with your higher self deepens, providing additional valuable guidance and wisdom in your life. Also, before connecting with your divine self, you need to connect with your higher self. (Your higher self will act like a bridge.) And as explained below, using your higher self as a bridge to connect with your divine self involves a deeper level of meditation and introspection.

CONNECTING WITH YOUR DIVINE SELF

1. Prepare Your Meditation Space

Find a quiet and comfortable place where you won't be disturbed. Sit in a relaxed and upright position, close your eyes, and take a few deep breaths to center yourself.

2. Connect with Your Higher Self

Begin with the meditation technique previously described to connect with your higher self. Imagine walking through your inner garden or serene place and meeting your higher self at a door or gate.

3. Set the Intention

While in the presence of your higher self, express your intention to connect with your divine self. You might silently state something like, "I seek to connect with my divine self, the highest aspect of my consciousness."

4. Merge with Your Higher Self

Visualize yourself merging or becoming one with your higher self. Imagine a powerful and harmonious blending of your energies. Feel a sense of unity and oneness.

5. Expand Your Awareness

With this merged state, expand your awareness beyond your individual self. Imagine your consciousness expanding like ripples in a pond and reaching out to connect with the universal or cosmic consciousness.

6. Seek Divine Guidance

In this expanded state of consciousness, you can seek guidance, wisdom, or connection with the divine. Ask questions or simply be receptive to any insights or experiences that may arise.

7. Let Go of Ego

Release any ego-based thoughts, doubts, or fears, which may interfere with your connection to the divine. Surrender to the experience and trust the process.

8. Experience Unity

As you connect with your divine self, you may experience a profound sense of unity with all of existence. This can be a deeply spiritual and transformative experience.

9. Be Receptive

Be open to whatever unfolds during this meditation. Messages or insights may come as feelings, images, words, or a deep sense of knowing.

10. Gratitude and Closure

Express gratitude to your higher self and the divine for this connection and guidance. Slowly return your awareness to your physical body, keeping a sense of unity and connection as you do so.

11. Journal Your Experience

After the meditation, take some time to write down your experiences, insights, and any messages received during the meditation. Remember that connecting with your divine self through your higher self is a deeply personal and spiritual journey. It may require practice and patience, and the experiences can vary from person to person. Regular meditation and self-reflection can help you strengthen this connection over time and deepen your understanding of your own divine nature and the interconnectedness of all things.

With time and practice, you will be able to connect with your higher self and divine self without completing a meditation. You will be able to just close your eyes and find the connection that you have developed. Once you have that connection, you can even state an intention with your higher self or divine self before entering the sleep state. You will be able to ask for guidance and for answers while asleep. This is why journaling could become an important part of your practice. With journaling, you will be able to see how much your consciousness has grown in your understanding of the universe and the importance your consciousness has within it.

While transcendence is not the ultimate purpose of every one of you, attempting to reach transcendence is helpful to every consciousness. Transcendence is about moving beyond the limitations of the ordinary, whether those limitations are physical, cognitive, emotional, or spiritual. It often involves a sense of going beyond the self or the mundane to connect with something greater, whether it is a higher reality, deeper understanding, or heightened state of consciousness.

I would like to take this opportunity to touch on a subject that has caused so much animosity and hatred among humans: religion. The universal message of all religions, while expressed in various ways and through diverse beliefs and practices, often revolves around common themes and principles that guide human behavior, foster spiritual growth, and provide a sense of purpose and meaning in life. It astounds me that humans continue to use religion as a source of hatred and self-righteousness. When you look at each religion, there are some key universal messages (none of which are hatred or self-righteousness).

1. Love and Compassion

Many religions emphasize the importance of love, compassion, and kindness toward all living beings. They teach that by showing love and empathy, individuals can create harmonious relationships and can promote peace.

2. Moral and Ethical Guidelines

Religions often provide moral and ethical principles to guide human conduct. These guidelines typically include concepts such as honesty, integrity, justice, and respect for others.

3. Transcendence and Spirituality

Religions encourage individuals to seek a deeper connection with the divine, the spiritual, or the transcendent. They often teach that there is more to life than the material world and that cultivating a spiritual dimension can lead to personal growth and enlightenment.

4. Faith and Trust

Faith is a central element in most religions, encouraging believers to have trust in a higher power, the divine, or a greater purpose. Faith provides hope, resilience, and a sense of meaning in the face of life's challenges.

5. Service and Altruism

Many religions call upon their followers to serve others and engage in acts of charity and altruism. These acts of service are seen as a way of expressing love and compassion through actions.

6. Unity and Oneness

Several religions emphasize the idea of unity and oneness. They teach that all living beings are interconnected and that recognizing this interconnectedness can lead to a sense of harmony and peace.

7. Forgiveness and Redemption

Forgiveness is regarded as a virtue in many religions. It is seen as a way to heal relationships and to find redemption or spiritual renewal.

8. Humility and Gratitude

Religions encourage humility in the face of the divine or the unknown. Expressing gratitude for the blessings of life is a common practice in many religious traditions.

9. Personal Transformation

Many religions offer a path to personal transformation and spiritual growth. They suggest that individuals can evolve and become better versions of themselves through their faith and spiritual practices.

10. Hope and Salvation

Religions often offer a message of hope and the possibility of salvation or liberation from suffering. This message can provide comfort and motivation in difficult times.

It is important to note that while these universal messages are common to many religions, each religion has its own unique beliefs, rituals, and cultural expressions. Additionally, interpretations of these messages can vary among different religious denominations and sects. While there is a shared core of values and principles, religious diversity exists. Individuals may find different ways to connect with and express these universal messages within their specific religious traditions.

Using religion as the motivation for murder, exclusion, hatred, etc. is manipulative and corrupt. Humans who decide to use religion for such purposes should just be ignored. Once realization sets in that other humans have become too intelligent to fall for such foolishness, religion will no longer be used for such purposes. And again, what it comes down to is transcendence and intelligence. Although there are some human minds that have not reached the level of others, those individuals who have a higher intelligence and who have attained a bit of transcendence should assist those individuals who have not. While no human enjoys the thought of being manipulated and used, the fact remains that the majority of humans are manipulated and used by others who want to achieve nothing other than the acquisition of power and money.

Spotting a phony or fraudulent religious leader can be challenging because they often use deception and manipulation to gain followers and to maintain authority. However, there are certain signs and red flags that may help you identify one.

1. Lack of Transparency

Phony religious leaders may be secretive about their personal lives, finances, or the inner workings of their organizations. They may avoid accountability and transparency.

2. Excessive Materialism

If a religious leader appears to be primarily motivated by wealth, luxury, or the accumulation of material possessions, it can be a warning sign. That person may use religion as a means of enriching himself or herself.

3. Claims of Special Knowledge or Revelation

Be cautious of leaders who claim to have exclusive access to divine knowledge or revelations, which no one else can access. Genuine religious leaders typically encourage seekers to explore and deepen their own spirituality.

4. Isolation from Family and Friends

Phony religious leaders may encourage or require their followers to sever ties with family and friends who are not part of their groups. Isolation from loved ones can be a tactic to exert control.

5. Demanding Excessive Loyalty

Leaders who demand unwavering loyalty and unquestioning obedience may be seeking to manipulate and control their followers. Authentic religious leaders often respect individual autonomy and freedom of thought.

6. Cultlike Behavior

Watch for signs of cultlike behavior, such as controlling what followers wear, read, or think and using fear or intimidation to maintain authority. Isolation from the outside world and pressure to recruit new members can also be indicators.

7. Excessive Focus on Fundraising

If a religious leader places an undue emphasis on fundraising or coercively pressures followers to donate money, it can be a sign of financial exploitation rather than genuine spiritual guidance.

8. Inconsistent Behavior

Pay attention to any inconsistencies in the leader's behavior, such as preaching one set of values while engaging in contradictory actions privately.

9. Lack of Accountability

Leaders who resist any form of accountability, whether from their followers, peers, or external authorities, may have something to hide.

10. Isolation from Critical Thinking

Phony leaders often discourage critical thinking and skepticism. They may label questions or dissent as signs of weakness or a lack of faith.

11. Exclusivity and Intolerance

Beware of leaders who promote an us-versus-them mentality, showing intolerance toward other belief systems or groups. Authentic religious leaders often advocate for tolerance and respect for diversity.

12. Abuse of Power

Any form of physical, emotional, or sexual abuse by a religious leader should be taken seriously and reported to the appropriate authorities. Genuine spiritual leaders are typically characterized by humility, integrity, transparency, and a commitment to the well-being and spiritual growth of their followers.

I apologize for having gone over my page limit. I'm going to say that it is OK because I waited for some time until my chapter began. (Ha, ha, ha!) I hope that you have enjoyed my chapter and that I provided you with the tools that you will use to further your transcendence and understanding of the universe. Thank you.

COMMENTARY BY ANUBIS

Thank you, Enki. This chapter really got to the heart of a number of topics. Up next is the final chapter of this book. And it is a chapter that some of you have been waiting for: Papa Legba. Papa Legba's chapter will not be for everybody. As he will explain, working with him will take you on a very interesting journey. I encourage you who are not familiar with him to read his chapter. You might not want to engage in some of the practices that he will provide, but his energy is powerful in a different way from some of the other guides that preceded him in this book.

CHAPTER 11

PAPA LEGBA

PAPA LEGBA

Papa Legba's Symbol

Greetings, children. I am the final guide in this book. I will thus say that the adage of saving the best for last is true. I am truly excited to begin. Some of you might not know who I am. I am a prominent figure in the Vodou (also spelled Voodoo or Vodun) religion, which is practiced primarily in Haiti and other parts of the Caribbean. It's also practiced in some African and diaspora communities. I am considered the most important and widely recognized spirit in the Vodou pantheon. My role is complex and multifaceted.

Before getting into who I am, I want to reiterate a concept that was touched on in the introduction of this book. Some people might be pondering, *I thought that Papa Legba is associated with the number one and therefore, that he should be number one in this book.* You must put all that information aside. There are times when I am associated with the number one—during a ceremony when I am essentially the gatekeeper. I am not a gatekeeper here (in terms of each energy coming through). Actually, there are many gatekeepers within this book. So for the purpose of this book, I am associated with the number eleven.

Getting back to who I am (for those who are not familiar with me), I am a prominent figure in Haitian Vodou, a syncretic religion, which combines elements of African, Catholic, and indigenous Caribbean beliefs. I am often considered one of the most important spirits or lwa in the Vodou pantheon. I am sometimes referred to as the gatekeeper or the crossroads spirit. I am an intermediary between the human and the spirit worlds. I am associated with crossroads, doors, and gates—both literally and symbolically. As indicated above, in Vodou ceremonies, I am invoked at the beginning of rituals to open the door to the spirit world and to allow communication between practitioners and the lwa. Often, I am depicted as an old man with a crutch, a straw hat, and a pipe. Humans contact me for my wisdom. Some humans understand that I have a mischievous personality. The symbol above is mine.

It's important to note that Vodou is a complex and multifaceted religious tradition. Beliefs and practices associated with me may vary among different Vodou practitioners and communities.

Let's discuss the number eleven. In numerology, eleven is considered a master number. Master numbers are those double-digit numbers that are thought to possess special vibrational frequencies and heightened spiritual significance. They are not reduced to a single-digit number, unlike most other numbers in numerology. The number eleven is often associated with qualities such as intuition, insight, spiritual enlightenment, and psychic abilities.

One of the key attributes of the number eleven is its connection to intuition and spiritual awakening. It is seen as a number that encourages individuals to trust their inner wisdom and to follow their spiritual paths. Those of you who picked this number (and me as your guide) likely possess a strong sense of intuition and a heightened level of awareness. You may be drawn to spiritual practices, meditation, and the exploration of higher consciousness.

In spiritual and esoteric traditions, eleven is often associated with the idea of alignment and balance. It is seen as a symbol of the connection between the spiritual and material worlds. The two ones in eleven are thought to represent duality and the need to find harmony between opposing forces. This idea of balance and alignment is echoed in various aspects of human existence, from the balance between light and dark to the equilibrium between the conscious and unconscious mind.

The number eleven has also been linked to the concept of synchronicity, which is the belief in meaningful coincidences. If you repeatedly encounter the number eleven in your life, you may interpret it as a sign that you are on the right path or that you are in sync with the universe.

In popular culture, the number eleven has made its mark as well. In numerology, the year 2011 was seen as a particularly significant time for spiritual growth and transformation, as it contained the master number eleven. Additionally, in the realm of entertainment, the number eleven gained prominence with *Stranger Things* when the character Eleven possessed supernatural abilities and played a central role in the story.

In Tarot-card readings, the number eleven holds special significance, as it is associated with two major arcana cards: The Justice card (Card eleven) and The Strength card (Card Eight). In some decks, it is numbered as eleven to maintain consistency with the Rider-Waite Tarot deck.

The Justice card typically features a figure holding a sword and a set of scales. It represents the concept of balance, fairness, and justice. When the Justice card appears in a Tarot reading, it often signifies the need for fairness and equity in a situation. It suggests that decisions should be made objectively and that consequences should be meted out based on careful consideration of the facts. This card encourages individuals to act with integrity and to take responsibility for their actions.

While the Strength card is traditionally numbered as eight, in some modern Tarot decks, the Strength card is numbered as eleven to maintain consistency with the Rider-Waite Tarot deck. This card features a figure gently taming a lion. It represents inner strength, courage, and the power of the human spirit. When this card appears in a Tarot reading, it often signifies the need to tap into one's inner strength and to demonstrate patience and compassion in dealing with challenging situations. It suggests that true strength comes from a place of love and gentleness rather than brute force.

The number eleven in Tarot symbolizes a powerful alignment of energies related to justice, balance, and inner strength. It suggests that individuals should strive for fairness and ethical behavior in their actions while drawing upon their inner reservoirs of courage and resilience to overcome obstacles.

Indeed, the number eleven holds a rich tapestry of meanings and symbolism across various cultures, belief systems, and contexts. It is a number associated with intuition, spiritual enlightenment, balance, and alignment. Whether in the realm of numerology, spirituality, or popular culture, the allure of eleven continues to captivate human imagination and underscores the profound ways that numbers can shape our understanding of the world and our place in it. Ultimately, the meaning of the number eleven is as diverse and multifaceted as the human experiences and beliefs it touches upon.

While I am known within the Vodou community, I am underutilized. So within the context of this book, I will teach those of you who pick me as your guide how not to be afraid when your life is disrupted. Humans fear so much of the unknown. Fear is a universal human emotion, which has evolved as a response to threats and dangers and has served as a vital survival mechanism. While fear can be adaptive in certain situations, it is often considered a negative emotion when it becomes chronic or excessive.

Fear is deeply ingrained in the human psyche due to its biological origins. It triggers the release of stress hormones like adrenaline and cortisol, preparing the body for a fight or a flight response. In this sense, fear can be seen as a natural and necessary emotion for human survival. But when fear becomes chronic or persistent, it can lead to sustained stress. Prolonged stress has been linked to a range of negative health outcomes, including hypertension, cardiovascular disease, weakened immune function, and mental-health disorders such as anxiety and depression. Thus, excessive fear can harm an individual's physical and mental well-being.

Fear can also cloud rational thinking and impair decision-making. When individuals are driven by fear, they may make hasty, impulsive choices, which are not in their best long-term interests. This can lead to poor life decisions, such as staying in abusive relationships or making irrational financial choices. Excessive fear can also strain interpersonal relationships. Fear-driven behaviors like jealousy, possessiveness, and mistrust can erode trust and communication in personal relationships. This can lead to isolation and emotional distress for individuals and negatively affect families and communities. Moreover, fear can act as a significant barrier to personal growth and self-actualization. When individuals avoid challenges or opportunities due to the fear of failure or rejection, they limit their potential and hinder their abilities to achieve their goals and aspirations. On a societal level, fear can have far-reaching consequences. Fear-driven actions can lead to discrimination, prejudice, and social divisions. Politicians and media outlets can exploit fear for their gain, manipulating public opinion and fostering a climate of divisiveness and hostility.

Innovation and progress often require taking risks and stepping into the unknown. Fear can hinder creativity and innovation by discouraging individuals and societies from exploring new ideas, technologies, or ways of thinking. This, in turn, stagnates societal development.

Overcoming the influence of fear requires self-awareness, humility, and a willingness to embrace vulnerability. This is important because I am here to help you address the fear of the unknown and what happens after your physical human body dies. But before getting there, you must recognize fear in your daily life and figure out how to cope with and overcome those fears.

Death is one of the most common fears among humans. The fear of death is a complex and a deeply ingrained aspect of human psychology, which has been a subject of philosophical, psychological, and scientific inquiry for centuries. There are several reasons why humans tend to fear death.

1. The Self-Preservation Instinct

Evolution has hardwired living organisms, including humans, with a strong instinct for self-preservation. The fear of death is a natural consequence of this instinct. It drives humans to take protective actions that ensure the survival of their genes.

2. Unknown and Uncertainty

Death represents an unknown and uncertain aspect of human existence. The fear of the unknown is a common human trait, and death is perhaps the ultimate unknown.

3. Loss of Consciousness and Identity

Many people fear death because it entails the loss of consciousness and personal identity.

4. Attachment to Life

Humans form strong attachments to life, their loved ones, and the experiences they have. The thought of leaving behind everything they hold dear can be a source of anxiety and fear.

5. Fear of Pain and Suffering

Death is often associated with pain and suffering, especially in cases of illness or accidents. The anticipation of physical or emotional pain can contribute to the fear of death.

6. Cultural and Religious Beliefs

Cultural, religious, and philosophical beliefs play a significant role in shaping your attitudes toward death. Many religions and belief systems offer explanations and narratives about the afterlife, which can either alleviate or intensify the fear of death.

7. The Fear of the Unknown Process of Dying

Dying itself can be a fearful prospect for some because of the uncertainty surrounding the process. Fear of pain, loss of control, or the manner in which death may occur contribute to this fear.

8. The Fear of Regrets and Unfinished Business

Some people fear death because they worry about leaving behind unfinished business, unfulfilled dreams, or regrets about things they didn't do in life.

9. Social and Psychological Factors

Social and psychological factors such as cultural norms, peer influence, and societal expectations also contribute to the fear of death. People may fear being judged or stigmatized for discussing or confronting their mortality.

Facing your fears in life will assist you in coping with any fear of death. And I will get you there and will lead you through facing your fears. Before delving deeper into my abilities, I want to introduce my contract.

GUIDANCE CONTRACT

This Guidance Contract ("Contract") is entered into on _____ [date], by and between: _____[your name] ("Seeker"), who lives at the following address _____ _____ and Papa Legba ("Guide").

The purpose of this Contract is to formalize the spiritual or personal guidance relationship between the Seeker and the Guide. This guidance relationship shall begin on the date of signing this Contract and continue indefinitely.

The Seeker commits to being open, honest, and receptive to guidance. The Seeker agrees to actively engage in self-reflection and personal growth. The Seeker will respect the Guide's boundaries and expertise.

The Guide agrees to provide guidance, support, and mentorship to the Seeker. The Guide will maintain confidentiality regarding the Seeker's personal matters, as appropriate. The Guide will offer insights, advice, or suggestions to the best of his ability.

Termination of this Contract will be up to the Guide.

By signing below, the Seeker acknowledges that they have read, understood, and agrees to the terms and conditions of this Guidance Contract.

Seeker's Signature: _____ Date: _____

This Contract signifies the commitment of both parties to a mutually beneficial guidance relationship and outlines their understanding of their roles and responsibilities therein.

This contract is not to be taken lightly. Here's why. When you begin facing your human fears, it does feel a bit scary. Sometimes as you begin this process, you might want to terminate the contract. I will not allow that though. The reason is that you need to work through those feelings. Once you have surpassed and conquered your fears in life, you begin to feel more freedom and therefore, increase your frequency. When your frequency rises, you are able to understand and listen to messages from the universe. Consequently, you will begin to understand that there is nothing to fear regarding the transmutation of your consciousness.

Once you sign the contract, you will be able to hear and feel my presence. Some of you may have already met me. For those of you who have not, you should find a quiet space and focus on the word *freedom*. You will begin to hear and feel messages from me. To some, I might feel like a very strong presence. To others, I will present myself as a softer whisper. It depends on what will assist you the most.

So why did I use the word *freedom*? Freedom, when contemplated in the spiritual sense, transcends the physical and temporal boundaries that confine human existence. It delves deep into the realm of the soul and the psyche and touches upon the essence of what it means to be truly liberated on a metaphysical level.

Throughout history, numerous spiritual and philosophical traditions have expounded on the idea of liberation or enlightenment. Whether it's the concept of moksha in Hinduism, "Nirvana" in Buddhism, or "Salvation" in Christianity, these traditions share a common thread— the pursuit of freedom from the constraints of the ego, desires, and suffering. Spiritual freedom, in essence, is the realization that we are not merely our bodies, thoughts, or emotions but rather an eternal consciousness interconnected with the cosmos.

One of the central facets of spiritual freedom is liberation from the ego—the constant chatter of self-identity, judgments, and attachments that imprison the soul. In this state, the individual transcends the limitations of ego-driven desires and aversions, which leads to a profound sense of inner peace and serenity. Spiritual seekers recognize that they are part of a larger cosmic tapestry and that the narrow boundaries of self-importance dissolve in the face of this realization.

Material possessions and attachments are often seen as impediments to spiritual freedom. The ceaseless pursuit of wealth, possessions, and worldly success can shackle the soul to a never-ending cycle of desire and dissatisfaction. True spiritual freedom entails a detachment from the material world, not through renunciation but through a profound understanding that material possessions are transient and that they do not define your true essence.

Many spiritual traditions teach that spiritual freedom involves a deep connection or union with the Divine, the ultimate source of all existence. This union is often described as a state of profound love, bliss, and unity, where the individual soul merges with the universal consciousness. In this state, the boundaries of self and others vanish, and a sense of oneness with all creation prevails.

Another crucial aspect of spiritual freedom is freedom from suffering. This does not mean the absence of pain or challenges in life but rather a profound shift in your relationship to suffering. The spiritually liberated individual understands that suffering is part of the human experience and that it does not define his or her true self. They find a deep sense of equanimity and resilience in the face of life's ups and downs.

Attaining spiritual freedom often involves a paradoxical interplay of effort and surrender. While spiritual seekers engage in practices like meditation, self-inquiry, or prayer to cultivate self-awareness, they must also surrender their egos' need to control and manipulate outcomes. This delicate balance between striving for growth and surrendering to the Divine's wisdom is a hallmark of the spiritual journey.

In the spiritual sense, freedom is the liberation of the soul from the confines of the ego, material attachments, and suffering. It is the profound realization of one's true nature as an eternal consciousness, which is interconnected with the universe. Achieving spiritual freedom is a transformative and transcendent journey, which can lead to inner peace, love, and a profound sense of unity with all of existence. It is a timeless quest that beckons humanity to look beyond the surface of life and to explore the boundless realms of the soul. In this pursuit, you will discover that true freedom is not something external but a timeless and eternal essence, which resides within your very being.

So what are some things that frighten you? Some of you might start small. Perhaps you are afraid of spiders. Why? What makes them so scary? First, let's look at this from a rational perspective. Spiders play a crucial role in ecosystems and provide several benefits to both the natural world and human environments. Did you know that spiders are natural predators of insects and that they help control populations of various pests? They capture and consume a wide range of insects, including flies, mosquitoes, ants, and agricultural pests. This natural pest control reduces the need for chemical pesticides in agriculture, so it can help protect crops. Spider webs are engineering marvels. They inspire scientists and engineers in fields such as materials science and robotics. The study of spider silk and web construction can lead to advancements in biomimicry and the development of new technologies.

In the spiritual sense, spiders are often associated with creativity and artistry, particularly in Native American and indigenous traditions. The intricate webs they create are seen as symbols of the creative process and the interconnectedness of all things. In some cultures, spiders are associated with feminine energy and motherhood. The act of spinning a web is seen as a maternal gesture. The spider is sometimes considered a protective, maternal figure. This symbolism highlights the nurturing and protective qualities associated with the spider. In some mythological and mystical traditions, spiders are seen as weavers of destiny. They symbolize the weaving of fate and the interconnectedness of all life. Spider symbolism can serve as a reminder that our actions and choices have far-reaching consequences. In some cultures, spiders are seen as symbols of balance and harmony. Their eight legs and the shapes of their bodies can represent symmetry and equilibrium. Spider symbolism can encourage individuals to seek balance in their lives, both externally and internally.

Now, let's talk about this from another perspective. Almost every human has squished a spider at some point in their lives. Have you ever connected with a spider? Think about the last spider you squished. Think about the seconds before your shoe came down (or whatever squishing device you chose). In your mind, connect with that spider before the moment of its death. In your mind, recall squishing that spider. Now in this moment, do you understand the senseless decision to squish the life out of the spider? While a spider is small and relatively noncomplex, it is still a sentient being. Would it be so hard to just relocate a spider (with a glass and sliding a piece of cardboard underneath the glass)?

Figuring out and letting go of a fear like that (spiders), chips away at other fears. It also helps with boosting confidence. Now, some of you might start with something larger like the fear of being on your own. Having me as your guide guarantees that you will face those fears in this lifetime. The main thing that you will need to keep in mind is leaning on and communicating with me during the stressful times of facing those fears.

Perhaps you are afraid of flying. Some of you may have experienced a traumatic flight (and in that sense, your fear is from this lifetime). Some of you may have never experienced a traumatic flight, but you have no explanation why you are afraid of flying. In the latter instance, it is probable that you had a traumatic experience in a plane in a past life. So this fear may be conquered by revisiting that past life and coming to terms with that particular experience. And some of you may be able to connect with your divine self to see that past-life trauma. But some of you may need assistance in connecting with a past life. In that case, if you have signed the contract, and if you would like me to guide you through that particular connection, all you have to do is ask. Past-life regression is a highly individualized experience, and the depth and nature of the memories or experiences that emerge can vary widely. It's important to approach the process with an open mind and without expectations. Allow yourself to explore your subconscious mind and inner experiences at your own pace.

I am in no way saying that if you fear not being able to pay your bills, I'll configure your life so that you lose your job. I understand that to be able to continue your spiritual journey, there are certain material things that are necessary in life as you know it today. But what I will do is make sure that you are able to place the importance of that into perspective. For example, is it more important to make additional money or to continue a spiritual journal for the purpose of transcendence? I will make the answer very clear—not just the answer but also actively choosing the correct path.

I am not for everyone. I know that. And I propose that before you choose me, you enter into this relationship with your eyes open. Because if you ask me to be your guide, and you are not facing your fears, I will put things into place to make sure that you start.

By beginning this journey with me, some of you are beginning to face your fear of death. Kali touched on this, and I'm going to also. Karl Marx's statement that religion is the opium of the people is often used by atheists or others who would rather believe that their consciousness does not extend beyond this human life. I never know whether to laugh at those people or feel sorry for them. People who love to quote this statement are so full of fear that they would rather believe there is nothing beyond this one life than open themselves up to knowing that there is. They then have no understanding of the lessons they're here to learn. Then when their human bodies give out, the afterlife is a complete surprise. And because of their fear, they never felt transcendence in their human lives. The outcome is likely one of having to come back. It really is such a waste.

Understanding your fears and overcoming them in this life plays a crucial part in your next journey. By next journey I mean what you will do next. Perhaps being reborn as a human and having very few fears is next for you. Or perhaps you have graduated on to be a spirit guide. To be a guide, you must have enough wisdom and knowledge to give to the being you are guiding. And living afraid of so much (particularly the afterlife) just does not bode well for a human to then move on to be a spirit guide.

My chapter is coming to an end. I have appreciated the opportunity that this book has given me. I know I have an additional page, but I have said what I needed and wanted to say. I look forward to working with some of you. Those of you who have chosen me will shortly learn how smart and lucky they are.

COMMENTARY BY ANUBIS

Papa Legba is never one to disappoint. Now we go on to the conclusion. The conclusion will be a list of some of the people who will read this book. I will not be able to include every name. So if your name is not given, please email the transcriptionist, making sure to give your first name, and she will respond to you with a message from me.

CONCLUSION

As I stated above, in this conclusion, I will be giving individual readers messages. Please understand that this list is non-exhaustive. If you do not see your name below, just email the transcriptionist at <u>transmutation. mandala@yahoo.com</u> and provide her with your first name. She will get back to you with your message from me. Thank you for reading this.

Abigail/Abby: You're such an inspiration.

Addison: Being brave doesn't have to hurt.

Alice: You're closing in on something big.

Amelia: Nature is your safe space.

Amy: You are amazing.

Ava: Your potential is limitless.

Bella: You can do great things when you put your mind to it.

Charlotte: You're very gifted. You should continue to climb so that you can reach your full potential.

Chloe: We have worked together in past lives of yours.

Chrissy: You're able to heal yourself. You just have to believe that you can.

Christine: Knowing who you are and who you want to be is the key to a happy future.

Cindy: There is so much love for you.

Claire: You're able to make this world a better place.

Cynthia: Stop holding back regarding your ability to help others.

Emily: Your baggage is part of who you are; embrace it rather than run away from it.

Emma: I love, love, love you.

Faith: You are going to write a book someday.

Fiona: Beauty comes from within, which means you are beautiful.

Grace: Embrace all sides to yourself. Darkness eventually gives way to light.

Hannah: Standing out in the world is easy when you are true to yourself.

Isabella: You're able to access more of your brain than most.

Ivy: Surround yourself with people who understand you. They will lift you up (versus those who are jealous of you).

Katherine: Love yourself.

Kathy: You are awesome!

Kelley/Kelly: You are extremely empathic. Learn how to block this gift at times so that you do not get burned out.

Kellye: Breathe. Keep going. Breathe.

Kelsey: You are able to increase your frequency very easily when you want to.

Kyle: Change is inevitable. You are able to get through changes better than most.

Lily: I'm excited to work with you in the future.

Lucy: Your kindness is contagious.

Madison: You have the gift of being able to know exactly who you are. You are also able to help others figure out who they truly are.

Mary: When you get to know others, try harder to keep them in your life. Compartmentalizing loss can become a weight on your shoulders.

MaryAnn: Try looking up at the stars. You will be able to receive messages from them.

Mia: Be careful not to give too much of yourself to others.

Michele J.: Speak up when you see or hear something that you disagree with—your supervisor is not always correct.

Michelle: You dealt with a lot during these past few years. Things will get easier. Hang in there because your happiness is around the corner.

Nicole: You are such a positive light in this world. Don't allow others to dim it.

Olivia: You are highly intuitive.

Paige: Being successful in your career is wonderful, but you are here on this Earth to do more.

Rhonda: Your voice is important. Keep pursuing your goals.

Sally: You are an incredible person.

Sharon: Being a positive role model is important. Your decisions will determine your ultimate karma.

Sophia: You are sensitive to vibrations and can extract messages by queuing into them.

Stella: You are an inter-dimensional traveler.

Zoe: I'm sending you love.

Now here is a list of men's names. Again, this list is not exhaustive. If you do not see your name below, just email the transcriptionist at transmutation.mandala@yahoo.com and provide her with your first name. She will get back to you with your message from me.

Adam: Faith is a difficult concept for some people to understand. You have a way with words, and you are able to discuss this topic with others in a way that opens their minds to different possibilities.

Benjamin: While the past does not define who you are, you must still make amends.

Christopher: You have a gift—being able to stand up for what's right.

Daniel: Pay attention to your dreams because you're receiving messages.

Ethan: Your parents do not define who you are.

Frank: You have a unique way of looking at the world. You should share your perspective more.

George: Freedom is a state of mind.

Henry: Being positive may be difficult, but it helps when dealing with family members.

Isaac: Start realizing your full potential.

James: Removing your fear of the unknown is essential to becoming who you were meant to be.

Kevin: You have an innate ability to communicate with animals.

Kris: Believing in the unknown is not weak.

Liam: You're an inspiration to many people. Don't give up on understanding your gifts.

Matthew: Find your inspiration within your love.

Nathan: Measure your success by the number of people whose lives are positively affected by you.

Oliver: Use water to help generate, upgrade, and upload your sixth sense.

Patrick: Try recognizing humanity in the people who affect you negatively.

Quentin: Once you have accepted your gifts, you will be able to move mountains (figuratively).

Robert: I can't wait to talk to you about your job here on this side of the veil.

Samuel: Let people get to know the real you because the real you is amazing.

Thomas: Don't shy away from people.

Ulysses: You're close to having a breakthrough.

Vincent: You're a gunslinger.

William: You are loved.

Xavier: Home is anywhere you want it to be.

Zachary: You're on the right path. Keep going.

Milton Keynes UK
Ingram Content Group UK Ltd.
UKHW022138290424
441966UK00010B/185/I